Developing Students'
Multiple
Intelligences

by KRISTEN NICHOLSON-NELSON

SCHOLASTIC
PROFESSIONAL BOOKS

New York • Toronto • London • Auckland • Sydney

Dedication

This book is dedicated to my parents, June and Gordon, who taught me from a young age that there was more than one way of doing things and that my way was just as good and probably better than most...although they were and continue to be a tad biased. To my wonderful grandparents, Bill and Ina Williamson, who traveled from the shores of Northern Ireland with enough stories to capture my writer's imagination and plenty of love and laughter to cushion my young years. To my grandmother Gigi, who always believed I was a writer at the age of three and has stories and early projects to prove it, and to my grandfather Nick, who taught me what hard work really meant. To my brothers, Tim, Bill and Louis, who have given me proof time and again of the fact that we all process information and learn in different ways. This book would not have been possible without my interesting and very multiple intelligent husband Kevin, who loves me enough to set me free to follow my dreams with an umbrella of security and acceptance to shield me from doubts and rough days. Lastly, this work is dedicated to the thousands of intelligent students who sit in classrooms throughout the country hoping to one day have a teacher who will open up the world of learning and provide the challenges which their young hearts seek.

Copyright © 1998 by Kristen Nicholson-Nelson
ISBN 0-590-93101-6
Edited by Jeanette Moss
Cover design by Kathy Massaro
Cover photograph by Donnelly Marks
Interior design by LDL Designs
Interior photographs on pages 15, 27, 45, 48, 49, 54, 55, 56, & 74
by Marc Solomon. All others by Kristen Nicholson-Nelson

Table of Contents

Introduction

I've found that many of the books published on multiple intelligences (MI) are divided into nice, neat chapters, titled with each intelligence. Within each chapter are little treasures and activities that are specifically tailored to each intelligence area. If only teaching were that simple and straightforward. If only students walked into our classrooms with one or two strong intelligences stamped on their foreheads to help light our path.

Yet reality is murky. Reality sometimes—probably most of the time—is unexplainable and difficult to measure. In reality, educating young children means recognizing that each of them is unique, complex, and highly individualistic.

My journey as a teacher working with multiple intelligences has not followed a clear and concise path of identifying students' strong intelligences and concentrating on those. Instead, it has been a process of wading into murky waters and seeing children holistically and individually. It has meant training myself to recognize that students are intelligent in many ways and that their overall intelligence is based on the sum of all their intelligences.

For example, Susie is an excellent math student. But no student who excels in math sits down to tackle an assignment and only uses his or her math-logic intelligence. Students achieve by drawing on the rich resources of their multiple intelligences. They use intrapersonal intelligence when they recognize that they need a quiet place to do the math. And when they come to a difficult problem, they use interpersonal intelligence by asking the right person in the right way for assistance. Word problems draw upon students' verbal intelligence. Geometry and graphs require spatial intelligence. Therefore, we can't label Susie as a math-logic intelligent student but an intelligent math student.

My desire to avoid separating intelligences was bolstered when I heard Dr. Howard Gardner, the Harvard professor who developed the multiple intelligences theory, speak at a 1995 Multiple Intelligences Conference in Big Bear, California. In his keynote address, he focused on the need to help students really understand the concepts and skills they're learning. He warned against using multiple intelligences to label students and spoke about the importance of recognizing that students need all of the intelligences, interacting with one another, to achieve genuine understanding.

I left Big Bear that Sunday morning and drove straight to my classroom, where I proceeded to tear down the separate bulletin boards proclaiming each intelligence and displaying matching student work. I wanted to provide students with an environment that would help them see themselves as a wonderful amalgamation of intelligences—not one that would restrict their learning by labeling and separating their intelligences into inflexible categories.

I want this book to help guide other teachers through the complicated process of teaching with multiple intelligences. I started out to write a logical, sequential set of guidelines and ideas that would provide a detailed road map for those just starting their journey. Yet as I thought and wrote, I realized that there is no one road map. Your journey will be different from mine. It will be a unique experience based on your own beliefs and philosophies. I can only write about what has worked for me. Take what you like and leave the rest.

Did You Know...

Teachers and peers don't always recognize creativity and imagination in young children. In fact many children don't enjoy or excel in school, finding it boring and mundane. History is full of examples of people who didn't take, or weren't given, the chance to experience the joy of learning during their school years. Did you know that...

★ Albert Einstein was four years old before he could speak and seven before he could read.

★ Beethoven's music teacher once said of him, "As a composer, he is hopeless."

★ F. W. Woolworth got a job in a dry goods store at age 21, but his employers would not let him wait on customers because he "didn't have enough sense."

★ Leo Tolstoy flunked out of college.

★ A newspaper editor fired Walt Disney because he had "no good ideas."

★ Abraham Lincoln entered the Black Hawk War as a captain and came out as a private.

★ Louisa May Alcott was told by an editor that she would never write anything that had popular appeal.

★ Winston Churchill failed the sixth grade.

★ Isaac Newton did poorly in grade school.

★ Thomas Edison's teachers told him that he was too stupid to learn anything.

★ Wernher von Braun flunked ninth grade algebra.

★ Admiral Richard Byrd had been retired from the Navy, declared "unfit for service," when he flew over both poles.

A Boy Named George

The perspiration from fifth-grader George Williamson's palms moistened the pages of *Charlotte's Web* and made page 54 curl at the bottom. His eyes shifted from the unfamiliar words on the page to Mrs. Carlson as she glanced around the room looking for someone to read. George heard the rest of the students turn the page, and he quickly turned his page. Page 55 was full of people talking—George recognized the quotation marks—yet the words seemed to taunt him and shout, "You can't read!" He found a few words that he knew, yet there were so many larger, unfamiliar ones.

George sighed with relief when he heard the words, "That's enough for today." Only ten minutes until recess, the only time all day that George felt good at something. Mrs. Carlson interrupted his thoughts, "I'd like you all to take out a piece of paper and start a picture that represents what we've just read." George quickly took out a piece of paper from his binder. Besides being the best athlete in the class, he was also a pretty good artist. He leaned over to Mark and asked, "What are you going to draw?"

Mark shrugged and said, "Something to do with some spider, I suppose."

George rolled his pencil up and down his sweaty palm and stared at the blank piece of paper. Right before recess, Mrs. Carlson came by his desk. "George, I thought you'd have drawn something by now. You're such a good artist."

"Just wasn't sure what to draw," George replied.

"Could you stay in for a few minutes at recess? I'd like to talk to you about something," she said. George sighed and slumped down in his chair, knowing the teams would be chosen by the time he got out to recess.

After the last student left the room, Mrs. Carlson queried George, "Are you enjoying *Charlotte's Web,* George?"

"It's okay," he answered, "for a girl's story."

Mrs. Carlson grinned and repeated, "For a girl's story, huh? Well George, I've been thinking about reading a book with you, just the two of us. You can still read *Charlotte's Web* with the class, but your assignments will be from the book that you and I are reading."

George quickly replied, "Is it because I'm stupid?"

"Of course not, George. You're one of the most intelligent students I know. You're smart in so many ways. You're having a few problems in reading, but you'll catch up. I want you to choose a book to read, and we'll work together to strengthen your reading."

George thought for a while and said, "I'd like to read a book about basketball."

Mrs. Carlson smiled and said, "Basketball it is. Leave the rest to me."

The next day George found a book on his desk entitled *Michael Jordan.* He began thumbing through the pages and found pictures of Michael Jordan slam-dunking and flying through the air.

Developing Students' Multiple Intelligences • Scholastic Professional Books

"All right!" he whispered as he turned to page 1 and started reading. When he came to words he didn't know, he decided to skip them until Mrs. Carlson came over to help him. After the reading period was over, George placed the book on top of his desk so other students would see it.

Discovering the Multiple Intelligences Theory

There have been several Georges in my classes throughout the years—students who struggle in reading and language skills and have either shut down completely and stopped trying or have spent years learning methods to hide their weakness. Either way, these students' self-esteem is low, and their feeling dumb is a challenge for the greatest of teachers.

I've taught in Southern California for eight years and have been lucky enough to have taught all the elementary grades, with more time spent in fourth and sixth grades. One reason I decided to teach was to provide students with a classroom that would celebrate their individuality. Yet I was soon to discover the critical importance of setting rules and managing a group of thirty prepubescent children. With so many bodies in one room, I found that celebrating individuality had its price—my sanity. After a few years, I went into survival mode and was just trying my best to cover the curriculum and make the experience enjoyable for my students.

On my journey to a quick burnout, I had a student who changed my life without realizing it. Kevin was a sixth grader who hated school and sat stoically for most of the day. His eyes were dull and his enthusiasm reminded me of a pet turtle I'd once had. One day driving home from school, I saw Kevin playing in the street with his neighborhood friends. His eyes were lit up, and he was jumping up and down with unbelievable enthusiasm. At that moment I knew I had to change my teaching, and I went in search of a new way of looking at this unique profession.

It was during my search for a way to change that I first heard about the multiple intelligences theory. I became fascinated and tried to learn everything I could about the theory. At first I analyzed which intelligences I was strong in and how this influenced my teaching. It was as if someone had finally explained what I had always known about myself.

Next I turned my attention to my students. I knew instinctively that students who didn't excel in my classroom were still intelligent and bright. I also knew that students had many ways of being smart and that all of these ways worked together to produce an individual who could succeed in school and in life.

The multiple intelligences theory did not change what I taught, but it did change how I taught. Learning about the different ways students can be smart made me realize that if I chose different ways of presenting information and lessons, more students might truly understand what I was teaching them. I agree wholeheartedly with Gardner when he says that if a student is to understand deeply, he or she must immerse himself or herself in subject matter, learning to think of it and to approach it in a variety of ways. And to accomplish this goal we sometimes have to sacrifice broad coverage and embrace the less-can-be-more philosophy.

The History of Intelligence Tests: A Traditional View of IQ

The Binet-Simon Intelligence Scale, the first such test, was developed by psychologists Alfred Binet and Theodore Simon in 1905 in Paris. The French government asked Binet and Simon to create a test to assess which students would most likely succeed and which would fail in the school system. In the 1930s, Lewis Terman revised this original intelligence test and it was renamed the Stanford-Binet Intelligence Test. This measurement introduced the idea of an intelligence quotient, which is the ratio of tested mental age to chronological age and is usually expressed as a quotient multiplied by 100. Currently, the Stanford-Binet IQ Test and the Wechsler Intelligence Scale for Children (WISC) are the most commonly used tests to assess and label intelligence.

Traditionally the Stanford-Binet IQ test defines how a child's intelligence is viewed. If a child is strong in verbal-linguistic and math-logic intelligences, his scores on an IQ test will reflect this and he will be pronounced intelligent. The school system has relied heavily on the IQ test and, consequently, stresses the importance of verbal-linguistic and math-logic intelligences. Experience has taught us that students who can read, write, speak, and perform basic math and computer skills are much more successful in school and, down the road, in their careers. It's important to recognize that the multiple intelligences theory does not downplay these two intelligence areas. It simply provides teaching strategies to help students achieve in these and other areas.

One of the foundations of the MI theory is that education can be designed to be responsive to individual cognitive differences. Instead of ignoring or denying these differences in the belief that all students have, or should have, the same kinds of minds, education should strive to provide all students with learning opportunities that maximize individual intellectual potential. As Gardner says, "Know as much as you can about the kids rather than make them pass through the same eye of the needle."

Intelligence Redefined

The multiple intelligences theory was first published in 1983 in Gardner's book, *Frames of Mind: The Theory of Multiple Intelligences*. Gardner derived his theory from extensive brain research, which included interviews, tests, and research on hundreds of individuals. He studied the cognitive profiles of stroke and accident victims, prodigies, autistic individuals, those with learning disabilities, idiot savants, and people from diverse cultures. He concluded that intelligence is not one inborn fixed trait that dominates all the skills and problem-solving abilities students possess. Gardner's theory doesn't question the existence of a general intelligence but probes the possibilities of intelligences not covered by one concept. His research suggested that intelligence is centered in many different areas of the brain, which are interconnected, rely upon one another, can work independently if needed, and can be developed with the right environmental conditions. Gardner's findings shook the educational community, which had become very comfortable with the notion that intelligence was a singular, genetic quality, measurable by a paper-and-pencil test such as the Stanford-Binet or WISC tests.

The intelligences Gardner recognizes include: verbal-linguistic, math-logic, spatial, bodily-kinesthetic, musical, interpersonal, intrapersonal, and naturalist. Each intelligence area is demonstrated through specific talents, skills, and interests. The fact that these intelligences can be nurtured and strengthened has a monumental influence on how children should be taught for maximum learning and achievement.

Current brain research continues to provide information that we never dreamed of knowing, and the multiple intelligences theory is helping to add to this wealth of information. As Gardner continues to research and study possible intelligences, it's important for us to recognize that we're learning about a theory in progress. Though the multiple intelligences theory has powerful implications for the world of education, before discussing the ways it can be put to practical use in the classroom we must remember that it is not an educational prescription. There is no one way to use it in the classroom, and many teachers use it in a variety of ways very successfully. However, if we assume that the multiple intelligences theory is generally an accurate portrayal of human differences, we can also assume that some, maybe not all, kids may learn more easily through some modalities than others.

Gardner first proposed that all humans possess at least seven areas of intelligence, each related to a specific area of the brain. Recently he has added an eighth intelligence, and he continues to research other possible intelligences. He defines an "intelligence" as consisting of three components:

★ The ability to create an effective product or offer a service that is valuable in one's culture.

★ A set of skills that enables an individual to solve problems encountered in life. Gardner believes that "IQ is the capacity to solve problems and make things. It's the can-do part that counts."

★ The potential for finding or creating solutions for problems, which enables a person to acquire new knowledge.

As a result of my work in the classroom, I believe that the multiple intelligences theory can be used to motivate and inspire students and provide variety in how we present information and lessons. Through it I've discovered different ways of personalizing instruction to help make children strong readers, writers, thinkers, mathematicians, artists, musicians, scientists, and historians.

Gardner recognizes three main ways that his theory can be used by educators. These are by:

1. cultivating desired capabilities and talents in our students.
2. approaching a concept, subject matter, or discipline in a variety of ways.
3. personalizing education as we take human differences seriously.

Gardner provides this vision within his theory: "If you want to teach something that's important, there's more than one way to teach it. Multiple intelligences can be useful as an inventory." My purpose in the next hundred pages is to provide you with an inventory of ideas and strategies to help students learn and truly understand what you are teaching. Here you'll find anecdotes on how this point of view has worked for me in my efforts to teach students who are struggling in school. And you'll find hundreds of practical ideas to choose from for your classroom. The traditional Chinese saying "Let a hundred flowers bloom" is a wonderful theme for the use of multiple intelligences theory in the classroom. Begin slowly, find what works for you and your students, and then stand back and breathe in the fragrance of your beautiful, blooming flowers.

The Multiple Intelligences

Verbal-Linguistic Intelligence involves ease in producing language and sensitivity to the nuances, order, and rhythm of words. Students who are strong in verbal-linguistic intelligence love to read, write, and tell stories. They have good memories for names, places, dates, and trivia. Professionals who use this intelligence include writers, public speakers, teachers, secretaries, business and office managers, comedians, poets, and actors.

Math-Logic Intelligence relates to the ability to reason deductively or inductively and to recognize and manipulate abstract patterns and relationships. Students who excel in this intelligence have strong problem-solving and reasoning skills and ask questions in a logical manner. They can also excel in science-related logic and problem-solving. This intelligence can be seen in such people as scientists, bankers, mathematicians, computer programmers, lawyers, and accountants.

Spatial Intelligence includes the ability to create visual-spatial representations of the world and to transfer them mentally or concretely. Students who exhibit spatial intelligence need a mental or physical picture to best understand new information; do well with maps, charts, and diagrams; and like mazes and puzzles. They are strong in drawing, designing, and creating things. Professionals who use this intelligence include graphic artists, cartographers, draftspersons, architects, painters, and sculptors.

Musical Intelligence encompasses sensitivity to the pitch, timbre, and rhythm of sounds as well as responsiveness to the emotional implications of these elements of music. Students who remember melodies or recognize pitch and rhythm exhibit musical intelligence. They enjoy listening to music and are aware of surrounding sounds. This intelligence is seen in such people as singers and songwriters, rock musicians, dancers, composers, and music teachers.

Bodily-Kinesthetic Intelligence involves using your body to solve problems, make things, and convey ideas and emotions. Students who are strong in this intelligence are good at physical activities, hand-eye coordination, and have a tendency to move around, touch things, and gesture. Professionals who use this intelligence include actors, athletes, surgeons, mimes, musicians, dancers, and inventors.

Interpersonal Intelligence refers to the ability to work effectively with other people and to understand them and recognize their goals, motivations, and intentions. Students who exhibit this intelligence thrive on cooperative work, have strong leadership skills, and are skilled at organizing, communicating, mediating, and negotiating. (Remember that this intelligence relates to a person's ability to understand other people but should not encourage overemphasis on cooperative learning activities and is not always found in extroverts. In fact, some extroverts I've known are weak in this area as they talk over, around, and alongside others on a regular basis). This intelligence is usually seen in such people as teachers, therapists, salespeople, counselors, politicians, religious leaders, and business executives.

Intrapersonal Intelligence entails the ability to understand one's own emotions, goals, and intentions. Students strong in intrapersonal intelligence have a strong sense of self, are confident, and can enjoy working alone. They have good instincts about their strengths and abilities. (This intelligence is difficult to observe. The only way to identify it may be by watching students and analyzing their work habits and products. Also, it's important to be careful not to automatically label students who enjoy working alone or who are introverts as being strong in this intelligence.) This intelligence is highly developed in such people as philosophers, psychiatrists, religious leaders, and brain researchers.

Naturalist Intelligence is the latest intelligence added by Gardner. It includes the capacity to recognize flora and fauna; to make distinctions in the natural world; and to use this ability productively in activities such as hunting, farming, and biological science. At a recent conference, I heard Thomas Armstrong explain this intelligence as the ability to see the natural world from a larger perspective—an understanding of how nature interacts with civilization, the symbiotic relationships inherent in nature, and the life cycles of nature. Charles Darwin, John Muir, and E. O. Wilson are examples of people strong in this intelligence. This intelligence is seen in botanists, naturalists, and physicists. I have had first-hand experience in watching this intelligence at work in my family members and husband. Surrounded by botanists, landscapers, and naturalists, a simple stroll through a neighborhood can turn into a rich and exciting learning experience. Discussions of plant adaptations, geological formations, and animal-people relationships has opened my eyes to the wonder and complexities inherent in nature that my own mind does not process. In today's world, some students use this intelligence as they make acute distinctions among cars, tennis shoes, hairstyles, and clothing styles. Because the naturalist intelligence has been postulated so recently, I have not included it in many related activities or ideas. In the next few years, one challenge will be to develop activities to help students recognize and strengthen it.

Currently Gardner is researching the possibility of an Existential Intelligence, which has to do with the ability to ponder the nature of existence—who are we, why do we die, how did we get here. It is seen in those who can deeply analyze and think about things we can't see and questions that don't have clear answers. This intelligence might exist in the clergy, philosophers, and spiritual people.

Developing Students' Multiple Intelligences • Scholastic Professional Books

Eight Ways of Being Smart

Intelligence Area	Is strong in:	Likes to:	Learns best through:	Famous examples:
Verbal-Linguistic	reading, writing, telling stories, memorizing dates, thinking in words	read, write, tell stories, talk, memorize, work at puzzles	reading, hearing and seeing words, speaking, writing, discussing and debating	T. S. Eliot, Maya Angelou, Virginia Woolf, Abraham Lincoln
Math-Logic	math, reasoning, logic, problem-solving, patterns	solve problems, question, work with numbers, experiment	working with patterns and relationships, classifying, categorizing, working with the abstract	Albert Einstein, John Dewey, Susanne Langer
Spatial	reading, maps, charts, drawing, mazes, puzzles, imaging things, visualization	design, draw, build, create, daydream, look at pictures	working with pictures and colors, visualizing, using the mind's eye, drawing	Pablo Picasso, Frank Lloyd Wright, Georgia O'Keeffe, Bobby Fischer
Bodily-Kinesthetic	athletics, dancing, acting, crafts, using tools	move around, touch and talk, body language	touching, moving, processing knowledge through bodily sensations	Charlie Chaplin, Martina Navratilova, Magic Johnson
Musical	singing, picking up sounds, remembering melodies, rhythms	sing, hum, play an instrument, listen to music	rhythm, melody, singing, listening to music and melodies	Leonard Bernstein, Wolfgang Amadeus Mozart, Ella Fitzgerald
Interpersonal	understanding people, leading, organizing, communicating, resolving conflicts, selling	have friends, talk to people, join groups	sharing, comparing, relating, interviewing, cooperating	Mohandas Gandhi, Ronald Reagan, Mother Theresa
Intrapersonal	understanding self, recognizing strengths and weaknesses, setting goals	work alone, reflect, pursue interests	working alone, doing self-paced projects, having space, reflecting	Eleanor Roosevelt, Sigmund Freud, Thomas Merton
Naturalist	understanding nature, making distinctions, identifying flora and fauna	be involved with nature, make distinctions	working in nature, exploring living things, learning about plants and natural events	John Muir, Charles Darwin, Luther Burbank

Scholastic Professional Books • Developing Students' Multiple Intelligences

What Type of Learner Are You?

Many times our own childhood plays a role in the way we teach. We need an awareness of our own learning styles to learn more about ourselves as teachers.

1. When I was a child, my favorite activities and hobbies outside of school were:

2. My favorite subject(s) in school was:

3. My favorite teacher was . . . because:

4. As a child, I always felt I was intelligent in the following ways:

5. As a child, I didn't feel intelligent in the following areas:

6. School would have been better for me if . . .

7. I decided to teach because of the following reasons:

Chapter 1

Getting Started with Multiple Intelligences

Before teaching with multiple intelligences, I briefly introduce my students to the idea that they are smart in many different ways. For two or three weeks I give them activities to help them become aware of the different intelligences and of their many talents and skills.

I select two or three activities that explore the different intelligences each week and integrate these into a curriculum area. These weeks can be magical times in the classroom. During this time, it's important to stress that students have all of the intelligences and that these intelligences work together to help them solve problems and succeed. You may find that students will want to label themselves as strong or weak in the intelligences right from the start. Stress that multiple intelligences is not another "labeling" device, and help them see themselves as intelligent in many ways.

Since they're just becoming aware of the many ways in which they are smart, I try to avoid activities that encourage students to analyze their own strengths and weaknesses. I want them to assume that they are smart in all the intelligences and have the potential to become smarter as they use all of their talents and skills. Following are some of the activities I use to introduce students to the intelligences.

START-UP ACTIVITIES

1. Ways We're Smart

Ask your students to name the ways people are "smart," and record their ideas on a sheet of butcher paper. The list will usually be dominated by skills found in the verbal-linguistic and math-logic intelligences. This is a good time to point out that these intelligences are the ones most recognized in school and are very important, but that there are other ways of being smart. After the list is complete, discuss each of the intelligences, using examples. For primary students, use Thomas Armstrong's wording: word smart, picture smart, number smart, body smart, music smart, self smart, and people smart. Use nature smart for the naturalist intelligence.

2. Telling Tableaus

Tableaus are "frozen pictures" in which groups of students "freeze" or pose to act out a scene describing a multiple intelligence caption while you read the caption aloud. Before starting tableaus, discuss the skills necessary to be a good "freezer" (i.e., eyes staring blankly, no movement, frozen expression, etc.). Have students work in groups and give each group a caption. Captions can be something like "Interpersonal intelligence (or people smart) includes the ability to work well with other people, be a leader, figure out how people are feeling, and help settle arguments between people." Give students five to ten minutes to develop their scene and practice their frozen poses. Don't allow any props.

To begin the performances, have the first group come to the front of the room. Turn off the lights and have the other students close their eyes as the first group sets up their scene. When the scene is set, turn on the lights and have the students open their eyes. Then you read the caption. Continue through the tableau scenes until all groups have performed.

3. Reminder Posters

Brainstorm ideas for posters that represent all of the intelligences. Then have each student create a poster, labeling each drawing with the intelligence it depicts. After displaying the posters in the classroom, have students take them home and hang them on their bedroom walls to remind themselves of the many ways they are smart.

4. Television Drama

Prerecord a part of a television show that will interest your students. (For primary students, this may be part of a cartoon or a Saturday morning show.) Show students a couple of minutes of the recording and then turn it off. Discuss the intelligences the characters are using. Show more of the program and stop it at a critical point in the story. Have students work in pairs to brainstorm decisions the characters could make. Then turn the show back on to see what decision the character actually made and what happened as a result of that decision. Help your students identify which intelligences the characters used.

For example, I recently showed a group of second graders a segment of a Bugs Bunny cartoon. As Elmer Fudd closes in on Bugs Bunny, I turned off the video and elicited student's thoughts on what intelligences this crafty rabbit might use to escape danger. We then returned to the cartoon to watch Bugs make one more famous escape by talking his way out of the problem and using his bodily-kinesthetic intelligence to make Mr. Fudd pay. We ended the lesson by discussing Bugs Bunny's many intelligences. One student exclaimed, "He's the smartest rabbit alive!"

5. Character-Study Discussions

Talk about book characters that your students know. These could come from a book the class read recently—for example, James in *James and the Giant Peach*, or be a famous character in literature such as the wolf in *Little Red Riding Hood*. Ask students which intelligences each character is strong in and how each shows his or her strengths. You might discuss fictional characters on television or in movies. For example, Bart on *The Simpsons* and the Beast in *Beauty and the Beast*. On butcher paper display running lists of fictional characters who exhibit specific intelligences. Remember to write a character's name on more than one list whenever possible to remind students that we are intelligent in more than one way. You might also include nonfictional people such as past presidents and other famous or historical figures.

6. Board Games

Have each student create a board game that features the multiple intelligences. To give students ideas, show them some examples of games and discuss the rules of playing. Students have used well-known games, such as checkers and Monopoly, and changed them to include a multiple intelligences theme. One student developed a three-dimensional game that included seven layers. Students had to answer questions correctly about one of the intelligences before continuing to the next level (and intelligence). Once everyone has completed a game, designate a Game Day (or afternoon) for students to play one another's games.

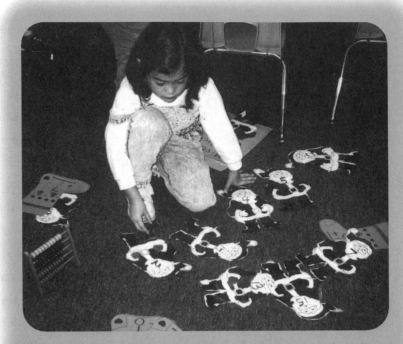

This student works most comfortably when she is given room to spread out her manipulative math game and an abacus.

After you introduce your students to the multiple intelligences, it's time to integrate these into your lesson planning by varying the way you choose to present information. Remember that you don't need to get hung up on integrating all of the intelligences into lessons regularly. I use them when there's a natural and easy integration into what I'm already teaching. By just becoming aware of the intelligences, you'll begin to incorporate them into your lessons and activities.

THE CHALLENGE OF WHOLE-GROUP INSTRUCTION

One of my greatest teaching challenges has been to teach a lesson to my entire class and still be aware of the many learning styles, strengths, and weaknesses at each individual desk. It would be ridiculous to sit with individual students and repeat the same lesson twenty or thirty times. But since individual students do need different types of experiences and activities to learn what is being taught, I find that most of the common behavior problems and disruptions I face occur during whole-group lessons. I'll frequently hear myself saying, "Don't talk when I am talking," "You should be listening, not writing," or "Stay in your seat."

I still use whole-group instruction, which often lays the foundation for the many small group and individual activities and projects that follow. But the multiple intelligences theory has helped me learn that I need to be careful to discern whether a student is truly misbehaving or simply isn't interested because his or her strongest intelligences aren't being called on.

For example, one of my students was constantly doodling on a piece of paper during my whole-group lessons. I asked Tommy to stop drawing while I was talking and to not doodle on the papers he turned in as assignments. But he didn't stop. As I got to know Tommy better and assessed his strengths and weaknesses, I learned that he was a highly visual-spatial learner and that his drawings usually related to what I was teaching. By questioning Tommy after a lesson, I realized that he had understood and retained most of what I'd taught. I began to accept his need to draw and was able to channel this interest into drawing pictures about the lesson for other students to review. I am not saying that all students who doodle are learning, but this student did teach me to take the time to consider different ways of learning before resorting to discipline.

The intelligence used most frequently in whole-group instruction is verbal-linguistic. Lecturing, writing on the board, providing worksheets, and encouraging note-taking and listening are important teaching techniques. I use them because they are the foundation of the school system, especially as students get older. The challenge is to integrate verbal-linguistic

Second graders flex their spatial and bodily-kinesthetic intelligences making a relief map of their school.

intelligence with other intelligences on a regular basis. By doing so, you will provide avenues for students to learn and understand using their personal learning styles. Not all lessons need to include multiple intelligences. Some lessons need to be taught in a direct and simplified manner. For example, many times throughout the year I read a book with my class just to read a good book or I teach a computation lesson using only math-logic techniques. Yet as my awareness of the different intelligences has grown, I now vary single intelligence lessons with multiple intelligence lessons for a balanced teaching style.

Chapter 2

Strengthening Your Teaching Through Multiple Intelligences

O ften the intelligences you use in your teaching are the ones you're strong in. It's only human to enjoy working in the intelligences that stimulate your mind. Still, it's important to be aware of the intelligences you use most in your teaching.

DEVELOPING SELF-AWARENESS

To begin, you can use the Teacher Reflection Inventory (page 158) in addition to studying your lesson planning book for the past couple of weeks. If you don't keep a plan book, write down the lessons you remember teaching. Now, note the intelligences used by students in each of those lessons. (Use the MI Lesson Assessment sheet on page 24.) As you begin to recognize which intelligences you tend to avoid or not use as much, you can start mending the gaps. Here are five gap-mending suggestions:

1. Team Teach. Find another teacher who specializes in the intelligences you'd like to strengthen. Begin to plan with this teacher, and schedule times when you can switch students so that both of you are teaching to your strengths.

Example: Mrs. Healey dreads PE time because she's not naturally athletic or interested in sports. Since she doesn't know the rules to many of the games, she finds herself in the middle of heated arguments between students. Her strength is in teaching science. She provides wonderful hands-on lessons that engage her students. To mend the gap in her teaching, Mrs. Healey asks Miss Horowitz, a strong PE teacher, if she'd like to team teach. The two teachers decide to rotate their classes each week so that Miss Horowitz teaches both PE classes while Mrs. Healey provides hands-on science lessons.

I work with a student to help him understand how math is used in geography. Once he calculates distances between two cities on a map, I'll ask him to spatially represent different ways to measure distance. Spatial learning isn't my strong suit: I had to make a deliberate effort to involve it in my teaching.

2. Use Specialists. Make more use of any specialists at your site—for example, the librarian, computer teacher, or resource specialist. They are usually happy to offer their services as knowledgeable educators.

Example: Mr. Smalley asks to teach sixth grade but is assigned second grade. He isn't up on the latest reading techniques and feels perplexed when working with squirmy second graders experiencing reading problems. One afternoon he asks to meet with Mrs. Leavitt, the school's reading specialist. He sits with her for two hours, and they review teaching techniques and research on helping primary students' reading. Now Mr. Smalley has more strategies to use with his second graders, and Mrs. Leavitt feels good about being able to use her specialty to help a colleague.

3. Recruit Guest Speakers. Send home a parent letter asking for guest speakers who have a particular skill or special knowledge. And solicit from community groups. For example, if your weakness is music, search for someone who is musical. You may be surprised at how many adults will want to come into the classroom to talk about and work with students in their area of expertise.

Example: Mr. Jorgenson, who teaches fifth grade, is two years away from retirement and doesn't want to be bothered with this "technology stuff." Yet he realizes that students need to learn about it. His class receives technology instruction once a week, when they visit the computer lab. Knowing that Tom Page, his student Mark's father, works for a computer company, he asks him to come and speak to the class about technology. Mr. Page is happy to come and has a great time talking to the students and answering their questions.

4. Fight Through Your Intelligence Shutdown. Okay, so you aren't good at physical activities, or at least you aren't interested. Yet knowing that a good number of your students need bodily-kinesthetic activities to be able to learn, you can begin to approach the subject through a different lens. Attend workshops, read books, and give it a try. The better you get, the more you'll enjoy it.

Example: Mr. Shephard hates math, has always hated math, and figures he will forever hate math. It was his worst subject in school, and he dreads having to teach math to his fifth graders. Mr. Shephard is experiencing an intelligence shutdown. After learning about multiple intelligences, he decides that even though he might not ever enjoy math, he can probably improve in it. He signs up for a hands-on math workshop and learns techniques to teach students math concepts using a variety of math manipulatives. Even though he forgets half of the activities by the time he returns to his class, he does remember several of them. The class loves the activities he tries, and Mr. Shephard's confidence in his math instruction is given a boost.

5. Call on Your Colleagues. Take a look around the staff room, and you'll find untapped resources to strengthen your weaker areas. For example, a fellow teacher who's strong in art and spatial intelligence activities can provide valuable advice and suggestions on how to incorporate this intelligence into your lessons.

Example: Mrs. Stevenson tends to ignore art at all costs. It seems messy, and she's never quite sure of how to organize the activities. Her next-door neighbor Miss Loren's room is adorned with beautiful art projects all year long. Mrs. Stevenson asks Miss Loren for some easy art project ideas to start out with and for advice on how to organize the projects. Once she has the ideas, she gives her students a wonderfully simple art project, which they love, and proudly hangs the finished projects in the room.

Multiple Intelligences Lesson Assessment

Lesson _____ **Date** _____

1. What intelligences did this lesson call on?

2. Which students seemed most interested and intrigued?

3. Which students seemed disinterested?

4. Were there any behavior problems during the lesson? Were these problems possibly related to an intelligence (i.e., talking, drawing, fidgeting).

5. What could I have done differently to make the lesson more interesting to more students?

6. What is another way I could have taught this material using different intelligences?

7. What was my favorite aspect of this lesson?

Though in teaching with multiple intelligences it's important to be aware of which intelligences are used in each lesson, it's not necessary to make a radical change in the way you teach. Instead, teaching with MI stretches good teaching into the realm of extraordinary teaching by including more ways for students to use all of their intelligences. Here's an example of how I taught a social studies topic before and after learning about multiple intelligences. The intelligences used are in parentheses.

Topic: Egyptian Pyramids
Grade: Sixth
Unit Time: Two Weeks

BEFORE MI	AFTER MI
Introduction. As a whole class, we made a list of what we already knew about pyramids. We read the pages from the social studies book that included information about Egyptian pyramids and had a discussion after reading. (verbal-linguistic)	**Introduction.** After visiting the school and public libraries, I collected 12 books that included information about the pyramids. I had the students form small cooperative groups and told them to imagine they were famous detectives. Their job was to uncover the reasons for and logic behind the creation of the pyramids and the uses to which they were put. (interpersonal, math, verbal-linguistic)
Class Activity. I gave students 40 minutes to sketch a pyramid using the pictures from the book. I instructed them to write three to four sentences underneath their sketches explaining what they had learned about pyramids. With the time remaining, they showed their drawings to the class. (spatial and verbal-linguistic)	**Class Activity.** After completing their detective work, I asked groups to design a poster that included the information they'd uncovered. Each group shared its poster and information with the whole class. A class discussion about the pyramids followed, including references to the information in the social studies book. (spatial and verbal-linguistic)

BEFORE MI	AFTER MI
Homework. I asked students to answer four questions from the social studies book. For extra credit, they could attach a drawing of the inside passageways of a pyramid. (verbal-linguistic and spatial)	**Homework.** I gave students two weeks to build a pyramid using mathematical measurements they could explain to the class. Before they began their assignment, we discussed how the Egyptians use math and engineering to build the pyramids. Students wrote a page explaining their building process. (math-logic and verbal-linguistic)
Language Arts Integration. I asked students to write a creative writing story that takes place in and around a pyramid. (verbal-linguistic)	**Language Arts Integration.** Students are told that they are lost in a pyramid and may not be able to find their way out. They are asked to make a cave painting with 10 to 15 pictures, which communicates who they are and what their life has been like until this point for future generations to learn from. (intrapersonal, verbal-linguistic, spatial)
Room Decor. We created a bulletin board that displayed the pyramid drawings and creative writing stories. (verbal-linguistic and spatial)	**Room Decor.** Students are able to volunteer to participate in a pyramid building group. These students use cardboard, paint, and a corner of the room to build a pyramid. (body-kinesthetic and spatial)
Conclusion. As a whole class, we examined the list we had made at the beginning of the unit. We made a new list of all the things we'd learned about pyramids. (verbal-linguistic)	**Conclusion.** Students design a game or a P.E. game with pyramids as a theme for other students to play. The only rule for the game is that it needs to include some type of "mood music" that will set the tone for playing a game centering on ancient death rituals. (spatial, music, and body-kinesthetic)

Developing Students' Multiple Intelligences • Scholastic Professional Books

The before lessons weren't bad lessons. I had used these techniques for several years, and the majority of students were involved and excited about pyramids. But the after lessons gave them the chance to use more than just their verbal-linguistic and spatial intelligences. And the after lessons didn't take much longer for me to plan or for the students to accomplish.

Ambuel Elementary sixth graders create a whodunit board game based on their knowledge of ancient civilizations.

TWO SAMPLE LESSONS THAT COMBINE INTELLIGENCES

As you plan more and more with multiple intelligences, it becomes more natural and takes less time. And remember, not every whole-class lesson or unit has to or should include all of the intelligences. By including two or three intelligences in most lessons, students are given the opportunity to learn in different ways.

The following lessons include detailed examples of how to use more than one intelligence to teach two different kinds of skills: multiplication and sight words.

LESSON 1: MULTIPLICATION

Memorizing the multiplication facts and understanding the concept of what these facts represent are a necessary foundation for further math learning, and that can be particularly difficult for students. The following unit uses several of the multiple intelligences and has helped my students truly understand multiplication. The activity suggestions are categorized by intelligences to give you an idea of which types of lessons can fall into the different areas. Each activity is likely to draw on more that one intelligence but is labeled according to the one it emphasizes.

Subject Area:	*Math*
Main Concept:	*Multiplication Facts*
Goal	*Students will learn all the multiplication facts*
Grade Levels:	*Grades 3–8*
Unit Time:	*3–4 weeks*
Materials Needed:	*white paper, counting beans, glue, counting objects, art supplies, volleyball or playground ball, multiplication musical tapes, journals*

MATH-LOGIC ACTIVITIES

Some students are natural math-logic learners and just need the opportunity to work with numbers and the time to memorize computational facts. For these students, numbers are interesting and solving equation problems is fun.

Bean Counting: Give each student several sheets of white paper, 50 beans, glue, and a color pen. To explain the activity, write 3 x 4 = 12 on the board. Explain that multiplication is simply repeated addition and that today they'll be using addition to learn multiplication. Underneath the equation, draw three large circles and put four X's in each circle. Explain that the first number in the equation tells how many circles they'll need and that the second tells how many beans need to go into each circle. Have students work together to count all the X's in the circles and write "12" next to the circles. Have several other examples for the class. Then write 10 multiplication equations without answers on the board. Ask students to choose whatever equation they like, draw the circles on their paper, place the beans inside, and count the total number of beans to get an answer. Have them glue the beans to their paper and write out the equation.

VERBAL-LINGUISTIC ACTIVITIES

Students who have strong verbal-linguistic skills often understand math better through narrative and words. Many of these students find numbers alone meaningless and boring. Look in the literature chapter for numerous books that can help them learn math concepts in ways that will interest them.

Creative Writing Scenes: Ask students to write short word problems that include the multiplication facts. Encourage them to create names and personalities for each number. For example, 8 can be Mr. Eight Snowman and 4 can be Freddie Four. Use the following examples to get them started:

Freddie Four ate three lemons and had a stomach ache for 12 days.

Mr. Eight Snowman built two houses for his family because he had 16 kids.

Fearsome Five dug five holes in his backyard to hide his 25 comic books from his little sister.

Nancy Nine went on a diet and lost six pounds a week until she weighed only 56 pounds.

VISUAL-SPATIAL ACTIVITIES

Students who have a strong visual memory will benefit from drawing or building activities. They'll learn their multiplication facts more easily once they can visualize them spatially.

Students use a computer program that stresses spatial and interpersonal skills to solve a mathematical problem.

Multiplication Art: Have each student select five multiplication equations that are especially hard to remember. Then ask students to draw a picture of the equation and the answer. Students can choose to draw a picture and put the equation and answer somewhere within the picture. For example, a drawing for 5 x 6 might consist of a boy who is wearing a shirt with the number 5 on it, standing in front of an apartment door with a 6 on it, talking to a woman who is celebrating her thirtieth birthday with a cake that has 30 written on it.

Multiplication Building: For homework, have students choose two multiplication facts that are difficult for them. Then have them build three-dimensional creations that use or depict those equations. For example, the equation 9 x 6 = 54 can be depicted by a model house with six rooms and nine objects in each room. Students should share their creations with the class without showing the equation. Students love to study these models and figure out the multiplication fact hidden within.

BODILY-KINESTHETIC ACTIVITIES

Students who are good at using their bodily-kinesthetic intelligence to learn benefit from movement and hands-on activities that help them remember multiplication facts.

Tableaus: Use student-created stories from the verbal-linguistic, creative writing scenes activity as tableau captions. Ask students to perform the frozen scene as the caption is read. (See Chapter 1, page 16, for Tableau instructions.)

P.E. Jump Rope: Have students work in pairs, and give one member of each twosome a jump rope. The student without the jump rope gives his partner a multiplication problem. The jumper jumps for each number in the problem and then jumps the correct amount of times for the answer. For example, if the problem is 4 x 5, the jumper would jump four times and say "four," then jump five times and say "times five," and finish by jumping 20 times and saying "equals 20." Then the students change places.

Multiplication Baseball: Divide the class into two teams and designate a first, second, third, and home base in the classroom. (For example, the pencil sharpener can be first base, the blackboard can be second base, and so on.) One group stands at the front of the room (home base) while the other group is seated. One student from Team A is "at bat," while one student from Team B "pitches" a multiplication problem. The pitcher must know the answer to their team's problem or it's an automatic home run. After the problem is "pitched," the student at bat gives the answer and moves to first base. This continues until three students answer incorrectly at which time the teams trade places. To make the game more challenging, divide the multiplication problems into "singles" (easy), "doubles" (moderate), "triples" (difficult), and home runs (extremely difficult). Students at bat can choose which type of pitch they want. You can decide how many "innings" time will allow.

MUSICAL ACTIVITIES

Students who naturally learn and store information through music will enjoy memorizing their multiplication facts through songs and jingles. Don't be surprised if you hear these students singing a multiplication fact during math time.

Multiplication Music: There are several tapes of multiplication-fact songs you can buy at most teacher supply stores. Play the song every day before math class.

Multiplication Jingles: Ask students to work in pairs to create their own multiplication jingle using one multiplication pattern (5×0, 5×1, 5×2, etc.).

INTERPERSONAL ACTIVITIES

Students with strong interpersonal skills learn their multiplication facts more easily and more quickly by working with other students than by working alone at their seats with a math book.

Partner Game: Have students work in pairs and provide one answer sheet and a pile of counters or chips for each pair. Have partners take turns quizzing each other. When a student answers correctly, he takes one chip from the center pile. The game is over when all of the chips are gone. Students count their chips to see who won.

Multiplication Talk Show: Invite students to the "Multiplication Talk Show," where they'll participate as the guest audience and/or the featured speakers. The show is moderated by Mickey Multiplication and the topic is "The Rough Life of Being a Multiplication Problem." Invite students to role-play multiplication problems after giving each number a personality. For example, Freddie Four may discuss how confused he gets when he has to play with Mr. Eight Snowman and that the last time they played a game, he caught Mr. Snowman cheating 32 times!

Surveys: Have students take a survey of 20 other students to find out which strategy helped them learn their multiplication facts more easily.

INTRAPERSONAL ACTIVITIES

Some students need quiet time to store the information they're learning. These students are good at finding ways to memorize information on their own and get frustrated at the busyness of group activities. Sometimes they don't mind working with others, but they know how they learn best and may need some time to work alone and "do it their way."

Quiet Time: Allow students quiet, uninterrupted time to study and memorize their multiplication facts. Make sure students have answer sheets or flash cards.

Multiplication Journal: Have students keep a journal during the time they're learning or reviewing their multiplication facts. Writing about which problems they've mastered and which ones are still difficult to remember reinforces their learning. Also ask them to evaluate which activities helped them learn the multiplication facts and to write down their thoughts about why.

LESSON 2: SIGHT WORDS
The following activity suggestions for teaching sight words may work for you. But there's no need to change what you do. These ideas may help you to broaden many of your own techniques to include more of the intelligences—not necessarily all of them.

Subject Area:	*Language Arts*
Main Concept:	*Sight Words*
Goal:	*Students will recognize twenty high frequency words*
Grades:	*Grades 1–3*
Unit Time:	*5 weeks*
Materials:	*word strips, index cards, art supplies, playground balls, permanent marker, electric piano (optional)*

Sight Word Suggestions*

the	and	an	was	are
by	is	on	see	have
but	from	at	not	can
that	or	of	one	we

* Sight words can change throughout the year.

VERBAL-LINGUISTIC ACTIVITIES

Introducing Words: On strips of butcher paper or word strips, write each of the 20 words, one to a strip. Introduce students to five words each week. You'll use all 20 words in the activities during the fifth week. Explain to students that they will be learning words that are used a lot. After introducing words to students, hang the strips in a wall pocket so students can see them throughout the day. Anytime one of the words appears in a book or someone says it out loud, have students walk to the pocket chart and point to the word.

Student Writing: Have students underline the "special" words each time they use them in their writing assignments. Older students can keep a Special Word Dictionary where they write these words.

Paper-Plate Spelling: Write one letter on each of a number of paper plates and give each student several plates. Have students stand if they have a letter that appears in a word you say. If several students stand up at the same time, acknowledge all of them as you reinforce how the word is spelled.

MATH-LOGIC ACTIVITIES

Counting Letters: To help students who need a mathematical connection to memorize the sight words, have them write each word, count its letters, and write the number of letters next to it. For example, students would write "the" and place a "3" next to it. An extension of this is to have students count the consonants and vowels. Students would write "the" and next to it write "C = 2, V = 1."

Categorizing Words: Give groups of students each a set of 20 index cards with one of the words written on a each card. Ask them to work as a group to categorize words that might go together. After they are done, have each group explain its categories. For example, students may feel that all the three-letter words or all the words with o in them go together. For many students, categorizing similar words will help them memorize word families. This activity helps to build and strengthen sight-word vocabulary as well as to increase students' awareness of phonetic similarities.

SPATIAL ACTIVITIES

Word Pictures: Have students write one of the sight words in large letters in the middle of a sheet of paper and then decorate the page with pictures and drawings.

Word Search: Write a short story that includes all 20 words, and make a copy for each student. Have the students highlight or underline all of the "special" words they can find.

A student begins to work on the spelling words which he has learned in the *Three Ducks Went Wandering,* using a white board so the teacher can easily monitor his progress.

Configuration Clues: Have students write one word at a time on a sheet of paper. After each word is written, have them draw a box around it so they can see how the word looks (e.g., tall letters, short letters). Older students can draw individual boxes around each letter.

BODILY-KINESTHETIC ACTIVITIES

Sand Letters: Fill several shallow tubs with sand. Students can work in groups and take turns spelling each word in the sand. Once their teammates verify that a word is spelled correctly, they erase it.

Playground Ball Catch: Using a permanent-ink pen, write the 20 sight words all over each of several red playground balls. Have students form groups of four and stand in a close circle. One student tosses a ball to another. The student who catches the ball reads the word closest to his or her right thumb. Younger students can read any word on the ball.

Stand Up/Sit Down: Tell students that you are going to be reading them a short story and that any time they hear one of the "special" sight words, they should stand up. After all students are standing up, signal them to sit down. Do the same activity with the story projected on a screen as you read so that students can see the special word being read.

Body Letters: Choose several students at a time to come to the front of the room and spell out one of the words by forming their bodies into the shapes of its letters as best they can. Their classmates can guess the word.

MUSICAL ACTIVITIES

Singing Songs: During singing time, take time to point out the sight words in song lyrics. You might also have students sing and spell the words in a familiar song. For example, the song Hot Cross Buns can be sung with the sight words. For the word "the," the song can be "T, H, E T, H, E. the, the, the, the, the, the, the, T, H, E…or etc.?"

Consonant-Vowel Spelling: Instruct students to spell each word out loud to a partner. Tell them to say consonant letters out loud and to whisper the vowels. This helps students become more aware of individual letters and memorize a rhythm as they are spelling. It can lead to a discussion of the patterns of vowels and consonants as they recognize that many words start with a vowel, others have a vowel wedged in between, and still others end with a vowel.

INTERPERSONAL ACTIVITIES

Group Spelling: Ask several volunteers to come to the front of the classroom. Pronounce one of the sight words, and have members of the group spell the word, one letter per student. Once students understand the game, divide the class into groups of two or three and tell them to whisper the spelling of the word you say. Remind them that they are whispering so that other groups have to rely on their own knowledge to spell the words.

Buddy Spell: Ask students to choose partners. Give each pair one set of alphabet tiles or cubes (or index cards with one letter on each card). One student says a word, and the other arranges the letters in the correct order. Once the word is correctly spelled, the students change places and continue until they've spelled all the words.

INTRAPERSONAL ACTIVITIES

Study Time: Give students a list of the 20 sight words to tape to their desk. Each day, give them a couple of minutes to study the words.

Journal Writing: Have students choose two words each day to copy into their personal journals. Ask them to write a sentence or illustrate a sentence that includes the word and then relate the sentence to something they enjoy doing in their personal time.

USING THE INTELLIGENCES AFTER WHOLE-GROUP LESSONS

There are certain times or specific units that require a large dose of verbal-linguistic teaching techniques (lecturing, reading, worksheets, etc.). The following eight follow-up activities use multiple intelligences strategies to provide students the chance to learn the material in their own way. They can powerfully reinforce learning as well as provide further challenges.

1. Multiple Intelligences Discussion

On the overhead or board, put the outline of a discussion that is central to the day's lesson. Start the discussion, pausing at certain points to ask students to use their multiple intelligences to do an activity that's related to the discussion. Students might think of a piece of music they could play, a physical movement they could perform, or a visual image they might draw.

> *Example: After discussing the building of California Missions for ten minutes, I stop and ask students to sketch a picture of the mission we're examining in our social studies book. After 10 minutes, I ask my students to put their drawings away as I continue reading and discussing. After another 10 minutes, I have students pair up and read the next page together and discuss what they've read. This type of lesson covers a lot of information in a very active way.*

2. Intelligence Workout Routines

For certain subject-area rote learning or memorization tasks, help students devise mnemonic devices based on the different intelligences. Some examples might include rap times tables,

Developing Students' Multiple Intelligences • Scholastic Professional Books

visual symbols for the parts of speech, body movements for science concepts, and so on. Then have students create an exercise routine they can use for practice.

Example: After teaching my students about the different forms of water molecules (liquid, solid, and vapor), I ask students to stand up and act out each form. I say a specific form, and they move around the room in a way that represents that form.

3. Unit Reviews

After you finish a unit, have students pair up in coaching teams to discuss, review, and pull the unit together. Ask partners to find a way to summarize the unit so that they not only review the individual parts but also understand the "big picture" of the unit. Coaching teams each choose an intelligence as a medium for the review. The summaries may take many forms—everything from murals to songs to mind maps to outlines to dances. The point is to be sure that students know the content of the unit and understand its overall meaning.

Example: We had just completed a unit on the Civil War. I gave coaching teams of three to four students two social studies periods to create a summary of what they'd learned and then give a brief presentation to the class. One team performed a short skit and another presented a team mural. All of the presentations illustrated the main themes and consequences of the Civil War.

4. Two-Intelligence Reports

Assign students a research report about specific information or content that the whole class has covered. Ask them to include at least two intelligences in addition to verbal-linguistic. In advance, ask them to turn in a written description of their report plan so that you can meet with students who may need help.

Giving children lots of opportunities to work in small groups builds interpersonal skills.

Example: My class completed the book Roll of Thunder, Hear My Cry *by Mildred Taylor. I gave students one week to complete a report about the social injustice theme in the book. The only requirement: their report must use three intelligences. At the end of the week, the reports all looked different. One student created a mural to go with her written report. Her report also included a class survey on prejudice. Another student wrote a report and gathered a group of students and directed them in performing a relevant tableau.*

5. Current-Events Critiques

Assign students a newspaper or news magazine to read. Ask them to look closely for examples of the different intelligences as they read various articles. Explain that most articles are based on more than one intelligence. Students should be reading between the lines for the "intelligence news," which may be different than the news being overtly reported in the article.

Example: I give groups of students a newspaper or a news magazine in which to search for articles that relate to the different intelligence areas. Students find sport articles for the bodily-kinesthetic intelligence, human interest stories for the personal intelligences, the stock market news for math-logic, and so on. I remind students that many articles relate to several intelligences, and I challenge them to find these kinds of articles.

6. Special Spelling Activities

Have students produce a newspaper, write and perform a short skit, write a song, or create a P.E. game using spelling words. After they've completed their activity, have them give a one-minute oral report on their project and how they learned to spell each word.

Example: I may ask students to write a song or poem that includes all the spelling words on their list. Or I might ask them to create a one-page classroom newspaper that uses each word in the context of a story.

7. Alternatives Solutions

After a whole-class study on a contemporary global issue or a historical incident, divide the class into small groups, one group for each intelligence. Have the groups think of alternatives from the perspective of their assigned intelligence. Then hold a mock United Nations meeting at which each group presents its recommendations.

Example: After discussing the destruction of the rain forests throughout the world, I asked groups of students to come up with a solution—each emphasizing a specific intelligence—that would help stop the rain forest destruction. An interpersonal solution was to form a panel of experts to address the problem. A math-logic solution was to make the public more alert by publicizing statistical data in support of the theory that the rain forests will soon be extinct.

8. Guest Speakers

After a specific unit or whole-class instructional time, invite a community member, parent, or colleague to speak to your class. Choose guest speakers who have experience relating to the topic or unit. For example, after a lesson on transportation or a unit on motion, invite a fireman or policewoman to discuss the important role vehicles play in their jobs.

Example: Let's say your class is learning about different government jobs and the role government plays in the lives of everyday people. You might invite a city councilman to speak to the class about his job and his view of government. After his talk, students can ask him questions and give their own opinions of the government's role in society.

Lessons Using Multiple Intelligences and Bloom's Taxonomy

A good way to ensure that your lessons have higher-level thinking and reasoning skills is to refer to the Bloom's Taxonomy Levels. In designing lessons and individual projects, I use a list of verbs that remind me of the different levels.

As you begin to design lessons that exercise the different intelligences, it's easy to fall into the trap of developing great lessons that don't reach beyond the knowledge or comprehension level. But by keeping Bloom's Taxonomy in mind, you can construct lessons that draw on all six levels of the taxonomy. Using it as a guide, you'll be able to monitor how effectively you challenge students' intelligences in each lesson. The charts on pages 43 and 44 will assist you in lesson planning.

Bloom's Taxonomy Verbs

The following lists contain verbs that can help you relate your lessons to Bloom's Taxonomy. By referring to these lists often in your planning, you can be sure that these lessons draw on all of your students' intelligences and all of their cognitive abilities.

Bloom's Taxonomy

In 1956 Benjamin Bloom, a professor at the University of Chicago, shared his famous "Taxonomy of Educational Objectives." Bloom identified six levels of cognitive complexity that have been used over the past four decades to make sure that instruction stimulates and develops students' higher-order thinking skills. The levels are:

Knowledge: Rote memory skills (facts, terms, procedures, classification systems).

Comprehension: The ability to translate, paraphrase, interpret, or extrapolate material.

Application: The capacity to transfer knowledge from one setting to another.

Analysis: The ability to discover and differentiate the component parts of a larger whole.

Synthesis: The ability to weave component parts into a coherent whole.

Evaluation: The ability to judge the value or use of information using a set of standards.

VERBAL-LINGUISTIC

Knowledge:	define, memorize, record, list
Comprehension:	clarify, discuss, restate, describe, explain, review
Application:	interview, dramatize, express, show, publish
Analysis:	interpret, compare, inquire, investigate, organize, survey, question, test
Synthesis:	compose, create, imagine, predict, invent
Evaluation:	evaluate, revise, deduce, infer, predict, correct, edit

MATHEMATICAL-LOGICAL

Knowledge:	recall, collect, label, specify, record, enumerate, recount
Comprehension:	describe, name, identify, locate, review, group

Application:	test, solve, calculate, demonstrate, show, experiment
Analysis:	analyze, interpret, scrutinize, investigate, discover, inquire, organize, examine, question, measure, divide
Synthesis:	invent, formulate, hypothesize, set up, systematize
Evaluation:	rate, value, evaluate, revise, select, measure, assess, estimate, score

SPATIAL

Knowledge:	observe, label, redraw, rewrite, copy, draw
Comprehension:	illustrate, express, explain with pictures, demonstrate, draft
Application:	dramatize, demonstrate, illustrate, show, prove, build
Analysis:	scrutinize, arrange, diagram, compare and contrast, graph
Synthesis:	compose, produce, arrange, design, plan, assemble, build, create, construct, imagine, originate, produce, concoct
Evaluation:	value, select, choose, judge, appraise, recommend, order

MUSICAL

Knowledge:	memorize, repeat, copy, recall, name
Comprehension:	recognize, cxpress, describe, translate into music
Application:	practice, demonstrate, dramatize, show, teach, perform
Analysis:	interpret, analyze, group, arrange, organize, differentiate
Synthesis:	compose, arrange, construct, create, order, produce
Evaluation:	appraise, judge, value, recommend, assess, order

BODILY-KINESTHETIC

Knowledge:	repeat all action, tell in actions, copy, follow along
Comprehension:	discuss, express, locate, play
Application:	exhibit, use, simulate, operate, show, experiment
Analysis:	sort, inspect, arrange, discover, group, organize, dissect, diagram, classify
Synthesis:	produce, arrange, set up, invent, build
Evaluation:	measure, decide, estimate, choose, recommend

Scholastic Professional Books • Developing Students' Multiple Intelligences

INTERPERSONAL

Knowledge:	repeat, define, recall, name, collect, tell
Comprehension:	describe, explain, discuss, express, report, retell
Application:	simulate, interview, employ, dramatize, practice,
Analysis:	organize, survey, investigate, inquire, question, sort
Synthesis:	set up, formulate, arrange, plan, propose
Evaluation:	decide, judge, appraise, conclude, infer, criticize, recommend

INTRAPERSONAL

Knowledge:	name, repeat, memorize, study
Comprehension:	explain, translate, restate, express, review
Application:	dramatize alone, visualize, solve, plan
Analysis:	probe, compare, contrast, investigate, dissect, question
Synthesis:	plan, design, compose, assemble, hypothesize, imagine, create, arrange
Evaluation:	infer, assess, value, judge, endorse

Developing Students' Multiple Intelligences • Scholastic Professional Books

Multiple Intelligences Lesson Plans

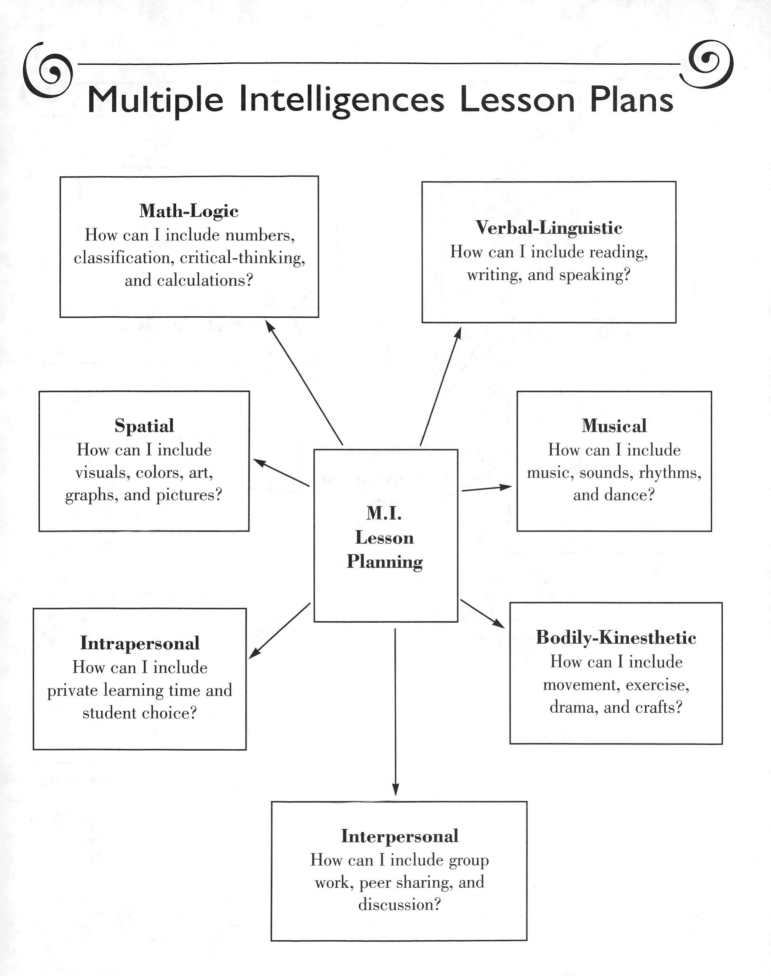

Math-Logic
How can I include numbers, classification, critical-thinking, and calculations?

Verbal-Linguistic
How can I include reading, writing, and speaking?

Spatial
How can I include visuals, colors, art, graphs, and pictures?

M.I. Lesson Planning

Musical
How can I include music, sounds, rhythms, and dance?

Intrapersonal
How can I include private learning time and student choice?

Bodily-Kinesthetic
How can I include movement, exercise, drama, and crafts?

Interpersonal
How can I include group work, peer sharing, and discussion?

Lesson: _____

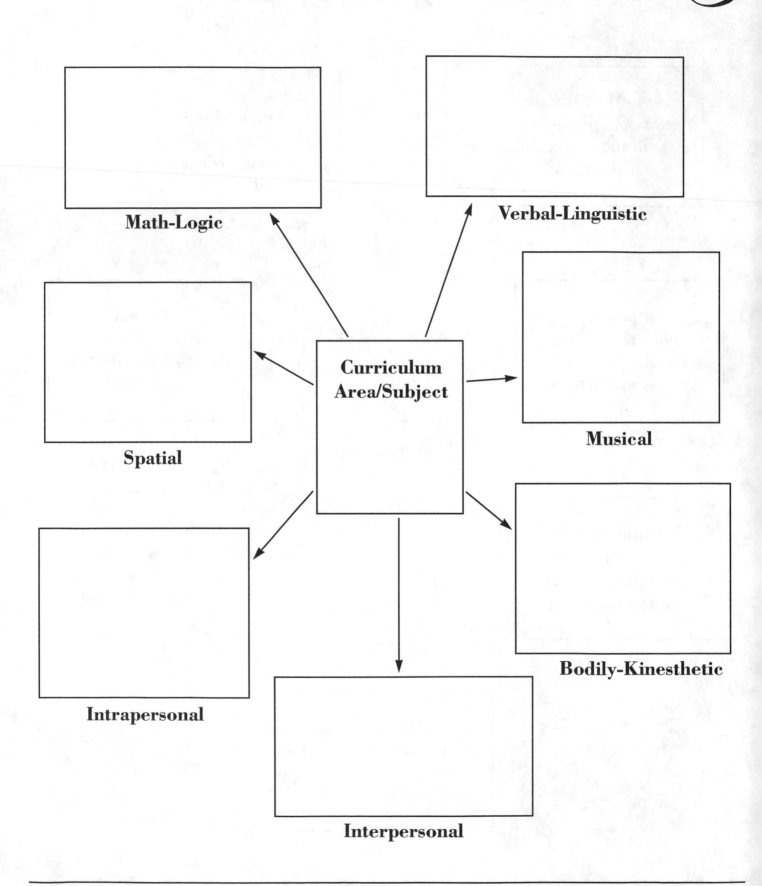

Math-Logic

Verbal-Linguistic

Spatial

Curriculum Area/Subject

Musical

Intrapersonal

Bodily-Kinesthetic

Interpersonal

Chapter 3

Small-Group Instruction Using Multiple Intelligences

S mall-group instruction gives you a chance to work with students individually and thus a better chance to assess their growth and development. Two strategies that work well for organizing small-group multiple intelligences instruction are learning centers and flex groups.

LEARNING CENTERS

Strategies and Organization

Small-group learning centers, classroom areas where several students can work together on a specific project or assignment, offer students powerful learning opportunities, both academically and socially. There is no right or wrong way to organize centers. In fact you may want to alternate your center format throughout the year. Some teachers using multiple intelligences centers prefer to create a center for each intelligence and keep them going all year. But this isn't practical for everyone. The number of centers you have at one time may depend on the size of your room, the number of parent helpers in your classroom, and the curriculum.

Strategy 1: Multiple Intelligences–Focused Centers

The main purpose of these centers, which each focus on one intelligence, is to awaken and strengthen the different intelligences. The activities and assignments provide students with opportunities to explore each intelligence in their own way, at their own pace. These centers can be especially helpful as you introduce the intelligences.

Strategy 2: Curriculum-Based Centers

These centers address curriculum information and skills, allowing students to learn and review through one or two intelligences. One center may offer verbal-linguistic and intrapersonal activities related to the book the class is reading. Another center may offer spatial and interpersonal activities related to the study of a period of history.

Strategy 3: Thematic Centers

Thematic centers are built around a theme being taught in the curriculum. The theme may be related to one curriculum subject (e.g., ancient-history architecture) or may cross curriculum areas (e.g., interdependence). Each center draws on one of the intelligences to explore the theme and the curriculum. For example, using the theme of ancient-history architecture, one center has students build a structure while another has students write a play about the building of the pyramids.

Developing Students' Multiple Intelligences • Scholastic Professional Books

MULTIPLE INTELLIGENCE-BASED CENTER RESOURCES

The following lists include materials and supplies you might use to prepare your centers. You don't need all of these items in each center, but it is important to have a variety of materials.

Verbal-Linguistic Resources

- reference books
- glue
- encyclopedias
- scissors
- computer
- desktop publishing software
- bulletin board
- thesaurus
- dictionary
- letter stencils
- sentence strips

- variety of paper
- newspapers
- notebooks
- trade books
- bookmaking materials
- magazines
- student-made books
- word mobiles
- writing utensils
- books on tape

Math-Logic Resources

- pattern blocks
- protractors
- unifix cubes
- balance scales
- tangrams
- tape measures
- puzzles
- rulers
- strategy games

- construction sets
- objects to serve as counters
- dice
- Cuisenaire rods
- calculators
- collections for sorting/classifying
- science equipment

Bodily-Kinesthetic Resources

- costumes
- puzzles
- miscellaneous props

- sand
- hats, scarves
- craft supplies

Scholastic Professional Books • Developing Students' Multiple Intelligences

Bodily-Kinesthetic Resources continued

- construction sets
- tools
- stacking blocks
- building materials/tools
- puppets
- sports books and magazines
- tactile learning materials
- scissors

Visual-Spatial Resources

- markers
- art prints
- crayons
- video equipment
- collage materials
- videotapes
- pastels
- graphic software
- colored pencils
- computer
- stencils
- puzzles
- rubber stamps
- graphs
- drafting supplies
- posters
- architectural supplies
- charts
- paints
- clay
- variety of drawing paper
- Lego sets
- picture library

Musical Resources

- tape recorder
- recording equipment
- headphones
- musical software
- tapes/CDs
- keyboard with headphone
- homemade instruments
- books on musicians and music
- instruments

Students listen to various musical selections before a discussion about how music can influence people's moods and motivations. Remind children that intelligences work together and most center activities include more than one intelligence.

Developing Students' Multiple Intelligences • Scholastic Professional Books

Interpersonal Resources

- large table for students to sit around
- group games and puzzles
- autobiography and biography books
- conflict resolution materials and posters
- tutoring activities
- group projects
- board games
- comfortable chairs/rugs
- writing paper

Intrapersonal Resources

- private, quiet place
- journals
- writing materials
- stories, books, and articles dealing with character development
- independent projects
- personal collections
- bulletin board/small chalkboard
- posters/pictures of individuals strong in this intelligence
- self-checking materials

A private, quiet place in the classroom is essential for students who enjoy working and learning alone.

MANAGING CENTERS

Managing a room full of students who are engaged in center activities can be challenging for the most experienced of teachers. Centers provide challenges such as physical activity, group talking, and the absence of direct adult supervision. To make center time run smoothly, it's important to be attentive to general management strategies that will prepare students to work in the centers.

STUDENT PREPARATION

Rules

Develop a list of rules that will guide your students' small-group learning. Center rules (see page 51 for a sample list) emphasize that centers are a privilege and that students must be responsible about following the rules in order to keep this privilege. Post the rules in the classroom or at each center, and take time throughout the year to review them.

Explanations

As each new center is developed, take time with the whole class to discuss the activities, materials, and end product or goal of each center. Many behavior problems can be avoided by ensuring that students know exactly what they should be doing in each center and what they are going to be held accountable for completing.

STUDENT GROUPS

Here are several options for grouping students to work in centers. Pay special attention to which students work well together and which seem to disturb each other. And remember that these groupings can be changed throughout the year.

Mixed Ability Groups: Form student groups that mix high, low, and middle academic abilities.

Mixed Intelligence Groups: As you get to know your students and their comfort levels with various intelligences, you can form student groups that mix intelligence strengths. For example, one group may have a student strong in spatial intelligences, one strong in verbal-linguistic, and another strong in the personal intelligences. To avoid labeling, I don't tell students I'm doing this. Yet this kind of group, with a mixture of talent and skills, has resulted in some of the most powerful learning projects and presentations I've seen.

Mixed Gender Groups: You might include an equal number of boys and girls in your groups.

Similar Intelligence Groups: When you form groups of students who are strong or weak in specific intelligences, the students have the chance to work with others who have the

Learning Center Rules

1. Do your very best work.

2. Use your quiet, inside voice.

3. Don't disturb others around you.

4. If you get up to retrieve materials, be courteous of others and don't disturb their group.

5. If you have a question, ask everyone in your group before you ask an adult.

6. When you complete your work, find something quiet to do at the center or at your seat.

7. When you rotate centers, quietly walk straight to your next center and start your work.

same interests and passions.

Random Groups: With this strategy individual students choose the center they want to work in, or they are assigned randomly to one by you. The students at each center form a random student group.

Temporary Groups: Have students work together for a short period of time and complete a specific number of centers.

Weekly or Monthly Groups: You may want to form groups that stay together for extended periods of time after you've had time to observe which students work well together. Allow each of these groups to choose a name and create a poster.

Students work together on a poster for a project on Egypt for which each student is required to add at least one item to the overall project.

Cross-Aged Groups: For combination classes or cross-aged classrooms, mix students of different ages.

CENTER-TIME SCHEDULING

Here are some scheduling options to choose from throughout the year:

Center Rotation

This system was first proposed by Bruce Campbell in his book, *The Multiple Intelligences Handbook*. The idea is to have multiple intelligences centers in the room at all times. You use a ten-minute mini-lesson on a specific topic to introduce students to information and activities. Students then rotate through the different centers, exploring the information using their various intelligences.

Specific-Days Center Time

Set aside specific days of the week or hours of the day for center activities. For example, each Wednesday and Friday afternoon might be designated as "Center Time." If there's not enough center room for all students to participate, have some students work independently at their desks on a project and call this the intrapersonal area. Depending on the center activities, have students rotate from center to center every 15 to 30 minutes.

Follow-Up Center Time

After you complete a whole-class lesson or a unit of study, use centers to review and reinforce the information students just learned. By rotating through centers based on the lesson, students can relearn the information in their own way.

Random Center Time

There are times in a classroom when natural lulls occur. These lulls can be ten minutes or longer due to time constraints or because you don't want to start an entirely new lesson with the time remaining. Use these random times for students to flow through the centers.

Students write a story together with the help of a computer program that allows them to add pictures to their stories.

MULTIPLE-INTELLIGENCES-BASED CENTER ACTIVITIES

You can use the following lists of ideas to develop center activities that awaken, strengthen, and nurture your students' intelligences. Use them as you introduce multiple intelligences to your students and periodically throughout the year. Remember to consider Bloom's Taxonomy as you design the activities.

Verbal-Linguistic Center Activities
- Book nook or library area for personal reading with comfortable seating
- Language lab with a tape player, cassettes, earphones, talking books
- Writing center with typewriter, computer, paper, pens, pencils
- Scrabble games
- Puzzle center where students create crossword puzzles and word searches
- Story-writing ideas and starters
- Letter-writing center where students can write letters to famous people or relatives
- Animal research lab where students learn about animals and insects
- Students invent a new P.E. game and describe it in words and pictures
- Newspaper center where students study and read the newspaper and then write an article for the class newspaper
- Tutoring Station where older students volunteer to help younger students with reading and writing

Math-Logic Center Activities
- Math lab with manipulatives and calculators
- Logic problems and mind benders for students to develop a strategy for solving and then solve
- Science lab with hands-on experiments and recording materials
- A variety of science books for students to read
- Enrichment math activities
- Monopoly game
- Students invent a measurement system
- Students design a playground game that uses math
- Measurement lab where stu-

This math-logic center challenges students to design geometry lessons which can be used to teach "blind" students geometric principles.

dents can measure objects and record their data

- Students design a way to teach a blind person geometric shapes
- Sample outlines, mind maps, Venn Diagrams, charts, and flow charts. Students choose one or two to organize a body of information
- Students write their own logic and word problems for other students

Spatial Center Activities

- Art area with paints, pencils, paper, etc.
- Student gallery with artwork displayed and explained in writing by artist
- Art history center with books and artwork from famous artists
- Visual media center with videotapes, slides, computer graphics
- Maps, graphs, visual puzzles
- Architectural center with pencils, rulers, large paper
- Building center with blocks for students to design buildings
- Pictionary game
- Students create flow charts or mind maps to explain what they have learned in the past week
- Students make up a math game using tangrams
- Clay center where students can make sculptures
- Students create a bulletin board
- Students make a map of their neighborhood, school, or city
- Students design a new playground for the school

Bodily-Kinesthetic
Center Activities

- Hands-on center with clay, blocks, crafts
- Drama center with an area for performances or puppet theater
- Tactile learning area with relief maps, different textures, sandpaper letters
- Open space for creative movement and drama presentations
- Books on sports and on

This spatial center provides an opportunity for students to sculpt their own chess set as they continue to learn this challenging game.

famous athletes and dancers

- Twister game with spelling words taped onto the color circles
- Students create scavenger hunts with a specific curriculum area in mind
- Juggling center with soft objects and a "how-to" juggling book. Students work in pairs to learn to juggle

Musical Center Activities

- Music lab with cassettes, earphones, and different types of music tapes
- Listening lab with "sound" items like different-sized bottles, stethoscope, and walkie-talkies
- Simon Says game
- Materials for students to compose their own songs and music
- Students create jingles that can be use for jump rope games
- Students demonstrate familiar patterns with patterned, repetitive musical selections

Interpersonal Center Activities

- Round table for group discussions
- Desks paired together for peer teaching
- Board games
- Books on friendships, family, communication, etc.
- Strategy ideas students use to plan a student government
- Question book full of questions to ask someone else
- Interview sheets to get to know someone else
- Students choose an important historical figure and write out a conversation they might have with that person
- Debate center with debate subjects and supporting information
- Index cards with common, school-related problems. Students work together to come up with solutions

A book nook is a popular verbal-linguistic area. Here, students collaborate on research.

- Index cards describing typical conflicts and a list of conflict management rules on how to negotiate solutions. Students role-play managing the conflicts
- Students choose a topic to become an expert on and teach the rest of the group in a five-minute mini-lesson
- Students interview someone in the group and write that classmate's biography

Intrapersonal Center Activities
- Study nooks for individual work
- Computer area for self-paced study
- Loft area where students can take a time-out
- The Ungame
- Journal topics for students to write on in their personal journals
- Students draw a picture that describes a mood or feeling
- Students write a poem titled "Who Am I?"
- Students set short- and long-term goals
- Students organize and add to their individual portfolios
- Students write their autobiography

CURRICULUM-BASED MULTIPLE INTELLIGENCES CENTERS

You can design curriculum-based multiple intelligences centers as places where students can explore the material and information they've studied in new ways. Some examples of curriculum-based centers follow:

CURRICULUM TOPIC: Using punctuation to avoid run-on sentences
GRADES: 2–6
Since this topic is already verbal-linguistic by nature, the center(s) will have students use a different intelligence to learn the same material.

Spatial Center: Prepare a page of narrative full of punctuation errors and run-on sentences. Have students become punctuation detectives and use different-colored highlighters to mark the various errors. For example, all run-on sentences might be highlighted in yellow and capitalization errors in blue. After they've found the errors, students should rewrite the page correctly.

Interpersonal Center: Provide a group of students with a paragraph that has no run-on sentences and perfect punctuation. Ask students to read the paragraph aloud, pausing when there is a new sentence. Then have them work together to rewrite the paragraph to include run-on sentences and read it aloud without taking a breath. This will reinforce what run-on sentences sound like.

CURRICULUM TOPIC: Forest knowledge and preservation
GRADES: 4–6

Interpersonal Center: Have a group of students design a "Protect the Forest Club" poster that provides information about forests, the animals, plants, and trees that live there, and the importance to the environment of keeping our forests healthy. Each student should contribute at least one idea or drawing to the poster. After the poster is complete, the group can hang it somewhere in the classroom and begin to plan the first meeting of the club.

Verbal-Linguistic Center: Have students write to an environmental club, political agency, or family member about the importance of taking care of our forests. Letters should include at least five factual sentences about what students have learned.

CURRICULUM TOPIC: Polygons
GRADES: 4–6

Bodily-Kinesthetic Center: Have each student use ten rulers to arrange different polygons on the ground. Once they have physically arranged the rulers, students sketch and label each polygon on a sheet of graph paper.

Verbal-Linguistic Center: Have students write a short story using personification to create characters based on different polygons. Each polygon should have a name and distinct personality that reflects the number of its sides and how it is most used or seen in real life.

CURRICULUM TOPIC: Geography: States and their capitals
GRADES: 5–6

Musical Center: Find a tape that has the names of states and capitals set to a tune. Place it in a center with a tape recorder so that students can listen and sing along.

Bodily-Kinesthetic Center: Write 20 state names on a beach ball. The group stands in a circle and tosses the ball to one another. The student who catches the ball reads the name of the state closest to his right thumb and names the capital. If he doesn't know the capital, the group can help. After students have learned the 20 states and capitals, prepare another beach ball to help with another 20 states.

CURRICULUM TOPIC: Organizing information into notes and outline form
GRADES: 3–6

Spatial Center: Students use the information on a topic they've studied to create a mind map—a visual representation using bubbles, arrows, and other graphic forms.

Bodily-Kinesthetic Center: Give students a large sheet of butcher paper and index cards. Have students write their topic at the top of the butcher paper and pieces of information on the index cards. As a group, students tape the index cards to the butcher paper, organizing the information as they go.

CURRICULUM TOPIC: The book *Island of the Blue Dolphins* by Scott O'Dell
GRADES: 4–6

Musical Center: A group of students creates a short song about the story. The melody and lyrics should represent the mood and events of the story.

Intrapersonal Center: Pretending they are the main character of the story, students write letters to their families explaining what has happened and how they feel about it.

Interpersonal Center: In a group, students design a model of the island and mark the spots on the island where important events occurred.

Scholastic Professional Books • Developing Students' Multiple Intelligences

THEMATIC-BASED
MULTIPLE INTELLIGENCES CENTERS

You can draw on thematic teaching to help your students explore and strengthen the multiple intelligences. The two themes with center activities described below are based on the premise that students have already had opportunities to research and learn about the theme. They provide a variety of ways to approach lessons through the multiple intelligences.

THEME 1: Endangered Animals

    Grade Level: K–5

    Materials:
- clay
- animal pictures
- poster paper
- art supplies
- writing materials
- tape recorder
- blank cassettes
- resource books about endangered animals
- tapes with animal songs (optional)

Spatial Center:
- Students make a clay model of an endangered carnivore and write a short paragraph telling key facts about the animal.
- In pairs, students design an advertisement that could be published in a newspaper to promote the preservation of endangered animals.
- Students build a three-dimensional habitat model for an animal of their choice.

Bodily-Kinesthetic Center:
- Students pretend that everyone at the center is a different animal, then role-play how each animal might react to meeting the others.
- Students perform a skit in which all of the characters are animals—some endangered and some not. The animals discuss the problems with being endangered.
- Students invent a P.E. game called the Animal Game.

Musical Center:
- In a group, students make up an animal song and record it on a tape recorder.
- Students write a poem or story about an animal and add animal sounds as they read it to other students in the center.

- Using a tape recorder, students record six animals sounds. Then they have another student listen and try to identify the animals.

Math-Logic Center:
- Students create a dot-to-dot drawing of an animal.
- Students classify pictures of animals into categories and explain the categories to other students at the center.
- Using a list of non-endangered animals, students rank the animals in order of those they think are most likely to become endangered and write a paragraph explaining their rankings.

Verbal-Linguistic Center:
- Students write a story in which the main character is an endangered animal who is trying to teach his family why the species is endangered.
- Students debate with their center group about the issue of wild animals being captured and put in a zoo. Should they or shouldn't they?
- Students write a short speech (2–4 minutes) about an animal topic that they feel strongly about. Topics might include how to take care of pets, endangered animals, or the similarities between animals and humans.

Interpersonal Center:
- Pairs of students write the names of ten endangered and unique animals on cards and test each other to see how many animals each recognizes from the other's list.
- Students write a group story (passing the story from one student to the next, each writing a sentence) about the difference between carnivores and herbivores. Then they discuss the benefits of being one type over another, explaining why their selection would help reduce the occurrence of endangered animals.
- In a group, students discuss the difference between land mammals and sea mammals, then summarize the important points in writing to turn in or share with the class.

Intrapersonal Center:
- Students write a story in which they become an endangered animal lost in a large city. They write about how they feel being lost and endangered and what they would do in this situation.
- Students choose an animal to observe for fifteen minutes. The time might be broken down into smaller segments if the animal is hard to observe. They write their observations and what they learned about the animal.

Naturalist Center:

- Students study an area or ecosystem where a specific animal lives and then teach the class how the animal survives in this environment. Examples might include alligators in a swamp, bears in the mountains or eagles in their nesting places.
- Students choose a plant that survives in a harsh environment and learn about how it survives. They write about what they learned and conclude with a "survival guide" for the family of plants. Examples: a barrel cactus in the desert or an oak tree in a winter climate.

THEME 1: The Future

Grade Level: 3–6

Materials:
- art supplies
- classified ads from a newspaper
- magazine samples

Spatial Center:

- Students design a home of the future.
- Students build a futuristic object that can be used in a classroom of the future.
- Students draw a map of the United States as they think it will appear in the year 2050.

Bodily-Kinesthetic Center:

- Students design a surgical tool that will be used in the future.
- In a group, students role-play a family scene in the year 3000.
- Students design a new P.E. game for future students to play.

Musical Center:

- Students design and play a musical instrument of the future.
- Students write a song that includes lyrics about the year 2050.
- Students select a contemporary song and tape-record a series of lyrics or a melody that they feel expresses something about society in 2015.

Verbal-Linguistic Center:

- Students research words or phrases that have recently become widely used—for example, Internet, World Wide Web, global communications, and beepers. Then they invent and write definitions for eight words they think will become widely used in 2015.
- Students write a creative story about getting lost during their first ride alone in a spaceship.

Developing Students' Multiple Intelligences • Scholastic Professional Books

- Students rewrite a famous fairy tale, adapting the story so that it takes place in the future. Examples may include Little Red Riding Hood traveling on a high-speed form of transportation to visit Grandma, or The Three Bears finding Goldilocks by means of their advanced alarm system, which displays a picture of their home even though they aren't physically present.

Math-Logic Center:
- Pretending that the President has announced that—due to technological advances—the money system will be changed in the year 2010, students create a new money system. They plan how to present their system to the President.
- Students create a time line for the years 2000–3000. They use the markings on it to predict what they think might happen.
- Students examine current "for sale" ads in the newspaper. They then write "for sale" ads for the year 2050.

Interpersonal Center:
- In a group, students design a magazine of the future, including articles and illustrations.
- With a partner, students make a list of problems students may face in the year 2050, then develop solutions to these problems.
- Students imagine they are running for President in the year 2050. Concentrating on the important issues of the time, they write a campaign speech that will help them get elected. They can hand in the speech or share it with the class or a small group.

Intrapersonal Center:
- Students write a story about being put in a time machine and suddenly transplanted into the year 2050. Then they interview another student in the center about what life will be like in the future, concentrating on how they feel about all of the changes they've written about.
- Students make a list of 25 things they're currently learning that may help them in the future.
- Students write a prediction about what their future may be like.

Naturalist Center:
- First, students research the current problem of traffic and crowds in our national parks and the environmental harm associated with these issues. Then, they create a list of ways to alleviate these problems for future generations.

• Students research a natural area that might possibly become a U.S. national parks in the future, then write a proposal telling why they believe the area should become a national park.

FLEX GROUPING

Flex Grouping bridges the gap between the two schools of thought on student grouping: ability grouping and mixed-ability grouping. Proponents of ability grouping believe that by grouping students with similar abilities, teachers are better able to tailor their teaching to students' levels. Opponents of ability grouping believe that it is a way of socially tracking students. They think that by putting the low-achieving students together on a regular basis, those students will come to see themselves as "stupid" or "slow." Research has shown that many of the teaching materials and techniques for low-achieving groups are substandard, putting these children into a cycle of academic failure. Critics of ability grouping also believe by putting the high-achieving students together, schools are raising a group of elitist children who won't be able to learn to work and communicate with all types of people.

Flex grouping provides teachers with the flexibility to meet with students who have similar academic needs, whenever the schedule allows these small-group instruction periods. Flex grouping can be used in all academic subjects, not just language and math, to guarantee that students are drawing on all their intelligences and getting their individual needs met. All students participate in flex groups from time to time, which reduces the stigmatization that has plagued the ability-grouping technique.

FLEX-GROUP:
A DEFINITION

A "flexible group" is a group of students who have similar academic needs at the same point in time and are formed so that a teacher can provide additional instruction to meet these specific needs and challenges. Because students' needs are constantly changing according to their progress and the academic area being taught, these flex groups change often. Since the groups are always changing, students are not labeled or stuck in high, medium, and low groups.

Developing Students' Multiple Intelligences • Scholastic Professional Books

FLEX-GROUP ACTIVITIES AND MANAGEMENT

The foundation of flex grouping is the belief that working in small groups, students will have any confusion about what they're learning clarified and the teacher won't have to reteach the lesson again and again. Flex groups are organized around the content area being taught in class, yet they

In one flex group, students are taught to associate specific vowel sounds with a color.

concentrate on specific skills and academic needs. Instead of reacting to what students "don't get," you can be proactive by preparing students for what they are going to learn tomorrow or the next day.

For example, Mr. Buffum's fourth-grade class will discuss the concept of "finding the main theme or idea" of a story in tomorrow's reading lesson. Mr. Buffum knows that six of his students will have difficulty with this concept. He asks the class to read the next chapter of the book individually before they read it tomorrow as a class but calls the six whom he thinks may need help understanding the concept to a flex group. Once the group is assembled and the rest of the class is reading, Mr. Buffum begins to read the next chapter with them. As he and the students take turns reading aloud, he teaches the main idea concept and together they talk about familiar stories and themes.

Later in the afternoon, the class completes a social studies lesson on the Civil War. Mr. Buffum asks the class to use a graphic organizer to explain the material covered in the lesson, yet he knows that three of his students will be able to complete the assignment easily. He calls these students to the back of the room, and as they work on their graphic organizer he asks higher-level thinking questions that challenge them to analyze and evaluate the Civil War.

Flex grouping is a time when students can receive individual attention and instruction without missing out on completing an assignment. It requires little extra preparation or grading by the teacher, yet gives the teacher a chance to work with students individually.

FLEX GROUPING EMPHASIZING MULTIPLE INTELLIGENCES

Form the groups by choosing a skill or curriculum area to reinforce a specific intelligence strategy. For example, if you have three or four students who are having trouble with reading comprehension, design a flex-group lesson that teaches comprehension using spatial intelligence. Invite these students to use graphic organizers to reinforce what is happening in a story.

As the flex group meets in another part of the room with the teacher, the rest of the class works in small groups to provide help and support to one another.

FLEX-GROUP ASSESSMENT

You can keep a Flex-Group Log to document which students have worked on which skills as well as their progress. This log is valuable to assess student growth and provide information to parents about individual student progress. A sample log page and a blank log for you to copy are provided at the end of this chapter.

One problem I had when I first began using flex groups was that not all of my students were getting a chance to work with me in a flex group. I'd been concentrating on the skills I needed to teach, not on which students were participating. As I assessed student's flex-group work, I noticed that several middle-ability students hadn't spent much time in flex groups. To balance this, I began to keep anecdotal records on a sheet of name-tag labels (30 to a sheet). I write each student's name on a label, and throughout the month, I write one or two sentences on each label noting which flex group the child worked in and assessing his growth there. I stick the labels in students' portfolios or onto a Flex Group Log. I make sure to use all of the student labels before starting a new sheet. This helps guarantee that all students get to work in a flex group.

Flex Grouping Log

Date _____

Group Members:

Skills Taught and Practiced:

Assessment Notes:

Teacher Small-Group Reflection Inventory

1. I usually use small-group instruction for the following purposes:

2. The most difficult thing about small-group instruction is:

3. The most frequent type of activities I use in small-group instruction are:

4. My small-group activities usually focus on the following intelligences:

5. The intelligences that my small-group instruction use the least are:

6. I can use my dominant intelligences to strengthen my small-group and learning centers instruction time in the following ways:

Chapter 4

Using Multiple Intelligences with Independent Projects to Individualize Learning

The theory of multiple intelligences provides a new lens with which to view students as individual learners. Combining the use of independent student projects with the MI theory has been one of the most motivating teaching techniques I've used. And it's also one of the easiest and most efficient. While students work on independent projects, I am provided with many hours to work with students on an individual basis. When I ask students at the end of each year which activities they enjoyed and which helped them learn the most, projects are usually at the top of their lists.

The time I gain through teaching with independent projects enables me to pay attention to individual differences and to match students to activities that will help them learn and understand what is being taught. I learned to stop comparing students' abilities and instead begin to work with each student individually.

A kindergarten teacher helps a student complete an individual project. Teaching young children to work independently provides them with a sense of ownership over their learning process.

And having more time has given me a chance to address another important aspect of learning: emotional memory. In July 1996 researchers at the University of California, Irvine, were able to show that a small walnut-sized organ deep in our brains called the amygdala goes into high gear during emotional events. Using PET scans, the researchers viewed brain activity in subjects who were shown exciting, emotional films and in others who watched dull films. Not only was the amygdala much more active in those that viewed emotional films, but weeks later subjects who had watched the emotional films were better able to remember details about what they had seen than were those who had watched the dull films.

This emotional-memory research is highly useful for us as teachers. We can make an effort to add an emotional element to our lessons whenever possible. I'm not saying we have to become actors and actresses and put on a show each day. And I'm also not advocating manipulating students' emotions to get them to "feel" something that they don't. But there are techniques we can use to increase the emotional impact of our teaching, at the same time making learning interesting, fun, and meaningful to students.

Teaching with multiple intelligences provides an opportunity to take a personal interest in students' lives and to provide them with learning experiences that have an emotional impact that they'll remember the rest of their lives. This hit home with me recently when I gathered together 50 of my former students and asked them to define a "great" teacher. The following point topped these high school students' lists: Teachers who were interested in me as a student and as a person. I asked students to explain further. The answers varied. Some students felt it was a teacher who was interested in what was going on in their lives outside of the classroom. Others felt it was a teacher who recognized their strengths and made a "big deal" of their talents, instead of "harping" on their weaknesses.

As I reflected on my students' answers, I thought of my fourth-grade teacher, Miss Nordyke, who took a personal interest in my life. I vividly remember her telling me that I was a good writer and encouraging me to write stories and poetry, which she would read to the class. At the end of year, she took all of my stories and bound them together. I ran home as fast as I could to show my parents my first published book. From that moment on, I became a writer and I've never looked back.

By knowing our students' strengths and weaknesses, we can tailor individual projects and activities to help students learn in their own way. One of my goals is to help students experience a crystallizing moment when they say, "Hey, this is really me. This is where I fit in and have talent." This gives students more motivation than I could ever provide, and these moments seem to come more often when I personalize education.

This chapter will discuss the use of projects and resource-based learning activities to help students experience learning for themselves. Students are encouraged to take some of the responsibility for designing their school experience. Through projects they learn to adapt the curriculum to their own needs through their multiple intelligences and to use these strengths to succeed in school. As they experience learning for the pure joy of learning, their emotional interest, intrinsic motivation, and hunger for knowledge soar.

THE PROJECT-CENTERED CURRICULUM

A couple of years ago, I attended a conference that steered me toward a project-centered curriculum. One session was on the "brain-compatible" classroom. Not really being sure of what "brain-compatible" meant, I bought Susan Kovalik's book, *ITI: The Model* (1994), which discussed eight brain-compatible elements for the classroom. These are:

- Absence of Threat
- Meaningful Context

- Choices
- Adequate Time
- Enriched Environment
- Collaboration
- Immediate Feedback
- Mastery

These elements were derived from years of research focusing on how the brain learns and what it needs to retain information and skills. I thought all the way home about how to integrate these brain-compatible elements into my classroom. I already felt that there wasn't enough time in a school day to teach all I needed to teach. Yet a few weeks later, I realized that by having students work on individual projects I could provide many of these key components to learning that their young "brains" needed and at the same time cover the curriculum and necessary skills.

Short- and long-term projects tailored to students' individual needs provide them with choices and a meaningful context and offer them valuable learning time for their brains to make sense of what they're learning. As students work on their individual projects, I can provide immediate feedback on an individual basis. This reduces the fear of failure that many students bring to the classroom.

Projects enable students to learn valuable skills with respect to research, working independently, assessing their own work, and the joy of learning in their own style. As we quickly enter the Information Age, there is no better skill for students to learn than how to access information and use the information in a practical and beneficial way.

There is no one right way to use projects in your class. Some teachers prefer to schedule time in the weekly schedule for students to work on projects. Others have students do the majority of project work as homework. Still others like to use a mixture of classroom time and home time.

TYPES OF MULTIPLE INTELLIGENCES PROJECTS

You can use various kinds of projects to enrich the curriculum, strengthen intelligences, and provide integrated and thematic learning opportunities. There's no need to use all of these types. Given the preciousness of classroom time, you may want to use only one or two types of projects all year. This chapter includes project ideas for the following categories:

Multiple Intelligences Projects: Based on one or several of the intelligences, these projects are geared to awaken and nurture students' intelligences. They are best used in the beginning of the year or whenever you are introducing students to the intelligences. You'll integrate your curriculum into these projects whenever possible, but the main focus is on the intelligences.

Curriculum-Based Projects: Based on the curriculum content areas, these projects are designed to enrich and teach students about a specific subject. They can be categorized by the different intelligences, yet the main focus is to provide higher-level thinking skills within the curriculum. Because the intelligences by their very nature are interdependent, it is difficult to design a curriculum project using only one of them. Most of these projects will be true "multiple intelligences" projects in which students can observe their intelligences working together.

Thematic-Based Projects: Based on the theme being used in the curriculum and/or classroom, these projects can be divided into intelligences. Yet like the curriculum projects, they will entail more than one intelligence.

Although students are working on their own projects, they are encouraged to ask their classmates for information and assistance.

Resource-Based Projects: Designed to provide students with opportunities to research a topic using multiple intelligences, these projects give students the chance to hone their research skills. They teach students how to navigate the myriad available sources in this Information Age. Resource-based projects can be easily integrated into other project categories.

Student-Choice Projects: These projects are designed and selected by individual students. You can help them by providing a list of project suggestions. And they can use the three categories—multiple intelligence-based, curriculum-based, and theme-based—as guidelines for designing their projects. Most students will choose from the project list, but some creative students will enjoy the challenge of coming up with their own project idea. Once they've decided on a project, have them write a project plan explaining what exactly they are going to complete. At the conclusion of the project, have them write a summary telling what they learned. (Copy the Project Sheet: Presenting What I've Learned worksheet included in this chapter.)

After creating a tableau performance depicting an era of Greek mythology, a student used his interpersonal skills to recruit and prepare classmates to perform his production for other sixth-grade classrooms.

PROJECT SCHEDULING

There is no one way to schedule projects with students. It takes jumping in and seeing what works with your class and curriculum. Here are some scheduling suggestions:

Regularly Assigned Projects. Weekly or monthly projects are assigned on a regular basis. All students have the same due date, though there may be some exceptions based on the complexity of a student's project.

Randomly Assigned Projects. Projects are assigned to all students whenever the schedule and/or curriculum permits. As you peruse your planning book, you'll identify times throughout the year when homework or class work slows down for whatever reason. These are wonderful times to assign individual projects.

Extra-Credit Projects. Projects are offered as extra-credit opportunities at the end of grading periods or interspersed throughout the year. The only problem with this is that the high-achieving students are likely to be the only ones to take you up on the offer.

Post-Unit Projects.
Individual projects can be a fantastic way to close a unit of study. After the unit is completed, assign projects so that students can show you what they felt was most interesting and what they learned. Require students to go beyond the information in the unit and expand on it.

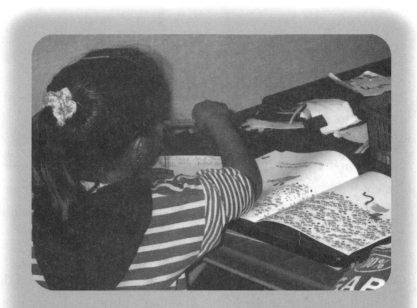

At a language center, a student writes a comment about what she has finished reading.

Schedule oral reports so that students can share their projects with the class.

Free-Flowing Projects. Different projects need different amounts of time to complete, but a due date for every project should always be set in advance. Meet with students individually to discuss their project and agree on the due date. To keep yourself organized and the students accountable, make a list of students' names and the due dates for their projects and refer to it regularly. As students finish their projects, have them sign up on a Project Share sheet. Then you can schedule their oral reports into your planning. Free-flowing scheduling is much like real life, and once students get used to the process, it runs smoothly.

PROJECT ASSESSMENT

The Multiple Intelligences Project Assessment Form at the end of this chapter offers a rubric for assessing students' projects. Share the form with your students so that they are aware of exactly how they will be graded. Be sure students are aware that the assessment of their project will be included in the overall unit grade. You might also want to hold individual conferences to go over the assessment. Skip any assessment criteria that doesn't apply to the student's work. Here are some ways to approach assessment of projects:

Letter Grade with Comments. Frequently I use the Project Assessment Form and place a letter grade based on rubric points on it. The most important part of assessment is providing feedback that explains why the student received the score—what the strong points of the project were and where there is room for improvement.

Student-Created Assessment. Before they begin, have students create their own assessment form to grade their project. Be sure to meet with students before they begin the project to discuss their form and approve it. This technique helps students become aware of what is included in assessment.

Teacher-Given Oral Quiz. After students have completed their projects and presented them to you or the entire class, give them a brief oral quiz about what they have learned. You'll be able to assess the depth of the students' work and whether they really challenged themselves. You might videotape (keep a tape for each student) these quiz sessions throughout the year so that you and the students can track their growth and progress in project work.

ASSIGNING PROJECTS

Assigning projects can take several forms. The most common is to assign all students the same project—for example, building a model or completing a book report. However, the concept of multiple intelligences is not truly captured by this method. Students need to draw on different intelligences and ways of learning and presenting information to truly understand the topics they are studying. Here are two other ways of assigning projects:

Project Lists. One of the easiest ways I found to assign projects is to create a list of possible projects for each intelligence. I encourage students to add to the lists, and they do add wonderful projects to my lists. For example, Heidi asked to add a project to the interpersonal intelligence list: interviewing city council members about what people skills they felt were most critical to succeeding in life. Greg ask to add a project to the solar system list: to find out how scientists measure the distance between planets.

Creating the project lists gives me control over the level of difficulty and curriculum area being covered in the projects, but frequently students will ask to do very advanced projects because they can choose to work in their strongest intelligences.

Teacher-Student Conferences. Another project-assignment option is to meet with groups of students to discuss projects you have in mind and to brainstorm for new ideas. You can focus these meetings on projects you want to include, but discussing—and contributing ideas for—their future work gives students a feeling of empowerment. And you'll be amazed at how quickly your project list grows.

PROJECT MANAGEMENT

I found that before I could have students work on independent projects, I needed to teach them independent-work-habit skills. Students strong in the intrapersonal intelligence have little difficulty with this, but most students need to be taught how to keep themselves on a schedule and not think of project time as free time. I'd always taught these skills, but now they had an immediate application and thus were more meaningful. My lessons focused on seven key skills:

1. How to set a project time line: I provide students with a calendar and teach them how to use the project due date as a starting point and then plan backwards. We note that a rough draft should always be completed three to five days before the due date to leave time for editing and last- minute changes.

2. How to self-assess and self-edit: I teach students the editing symbols and have them practice editing their own work.

3. How to behave during project time: We talk about how project time should be a very quiet time, and we discuss the need for movement and talking to be kept at a minimum.

4. What information resources are available: I take a few days to discuss available resources. One of the days includes a trip to the library to review how to find information and how to ask the librarian for help. We also discuss the resources available on the computer, including the Internet.

5. How to research a topic and organize information: I spend time teaching students how to take notes; use note cards, outlines, and graphic organizers; and how to synthesize and report information in their own words.

6. How to include the different intelligences in doing research: I provide the "Multiple Intelligences Information Suggestions" worksheet and talk with my stu-

dents about how the different intelligences can serve as a guide for information gathering.

7. How to present work creatively and neatly: I talk with students about their final presentation. We discuss neatness, spelling, punctuation, and presentation—for example, how to

I help two young students access information in the World History Center. After students compile their research, they are asked to organize it into the different intelligence areas.

create a project that is both visually appealing and professional looking. I show student work from years past to illustrate how final products succeed or don't succeed. I also show brochures and posters from businesses and the media as examples of final products.

PROJECT LISTS

I use projects in the beginning of the year to introduce my students to the different intelligences. Once they have a firm grasp of the intelligences and the skills each provides, I move on to projects that are curriculum- or thematic-based and use several intelligences at a time. However, I want to warn you that every year my students beg to return to the multiple intelligences projects. Once that happens, I use the MI projects as rewards and motivators.

As you begin using independent projects with your students, you'll begin to compile your own lists, which will include grade-, age-, and challenge-level appropriate projects.

MULTIPLE INTELLIGENCES PROJECT LISTS

One of my students, Tracy, upon completing a multiple-intelligence-based project, said proudly, "I never knew I was being smart when I played music." When I told her that music was one of my weaker areas, she beamed with pride and informed the rest of the class that she was smarter than the teacher.

When I first began using MI projects, I found that students would naturally choose from their strong intelligences. As time went on, I required them to complete a project from each list before revisiting one. Periodically throughout the year, I have students revisit these lists and complete a project.

I've provided generic examples in order to give you an idea of different types of projects that isolate the intelligences. I've categorized them into Bloom's Taxonomy to be sure that students are practicing advanced levels of thinking and reasoning. I start students with the knowledge- and comprehension-level projects to help them gain a general awareness of their intelligences and then move them along to the higher levels of thinking and reasoning to strengthen and challenge their intelligences. Remember that the curriculum can be included in these projects when possible, but the main focus is on strengthening the intelligences.

MULTIPLE INTELLIGENCES PROJECTS FOR BODILY-KINESTHETIC INTELLIGENCE

Knowledge Level
- Teach the class the rules of a game (e.g., soccer, hockey, football). Use diagrams and/or pictures.
- Research what "healthy living" means and explain it in a short report.
- Make a drawing of your favorite athletic event and demonstrate it for the class.

Comprehension Level
- Act out the relationships between the earth, moon, and sun as they revolve around the galaxy.
- Research a sport played in a foreign country and teach it to the class.
- Research two famous games played in recent sporting history. This can be the Super Bowl, the NBA playoffs, or any other famous game. Summarize each game in a brief essay to share with the class.

Application Level

• Using class members, demonstrate the rotation in the planets in the solar system.

• Demonstrate bicycle safety techniques for the class.

• Learn and teach sign language to the class.

• Learn about and demonstrate one of the martial arts.

• Find out what a younger class is studying and perform a puppet show for students about this topic.

Analysis Level

• Write and perform a skit or tableau that illustrates how a group of people from a certain period of history survived a crisis.

• Act out the movement of molecules in a gas as temperature and pressure change. Explain the movement changes to the class.

• Survey all your classmates to find out how they use their bodily-kinesthetic intelligence to help them learn in school. Make a graph that compares your findings.

• Categorize all the sports you can think of into "sport families." Make a chart showing your different categories and each sport included in them.

Synthesis Level

• Create an original dance to go with a poem.

• Invent a new team game and teach it to the class.

• Design a personal diet and exercise plan that will help you remain healthy and strong.

• Role-play an important event from history or from a book of literature.

• Develop a game of charades using characters from books and stories read in class.

• Create a tableau to depict a work of art.

Evaluation Level

• Demonstrate a hands-on science experiment for the class. After the demonstration, discuss what worked and what didn't work in the experiment.

• Have a debate with a group of students about the inclusion of girls on the boys' team in Little League.

• Compare the similarities and differences between the sports older students play versus those younger students play.

Developing Students' Multiple Intelligences • Scholastic Professional Books

MULTIPLE INTELLIGENCES PROJECTS
FOR INTERPERSONAL INTELLIGENCE

Knowledge Level
- Write an essay on "How to Be a Good Friend."
- Define what a good friend is and write it in dictionary language and form.
- Find ten quotes on friendship and write them down. Pass them out to the class.

Comprehension Level
- Write a group story in which one student starts the story and then passes it on. Write the story on a specific theme (friendship, family life, honesty, etc.).
- Write a team position paper on a current-events issue.
- Have each member of the group role-play a current national leader and have a meeting to discuss an important issue.

Application Level
- Write and illustrate a picture book to read to another class.
- Individually or with a partner, conduct a science experiment to teach the class a concept.
- Perform a group skit to present a science concept.

Analysis Level
- Create an advertisement for a company that offers assistance to student groups who are having problems working together.
- Analyze how first-grade friendships are different from fifth-grade friendships.
- Using a family tree to help you remember all of your relatives, make a diagram of your family.

Synthesis Level
- Choose an important historical figure and role-play a conversation with him or her.
- With your group, develop a Reader's Theater script and present it to the class.
- Learn or invent a noncompetitive game to teach to the class.
- Choose two different grade levels and design different ways to teach them the same math lesson.
- As a group, design and create a museum exhibit featuring important artifacts from a period we're learning about.

Scholastic Professional Books • Developing Students' Multiple Intelligences

• Create a picture dictionary of feelings, attitudes, and/or body language.

• Organize a "Just Say NO to Drugs" club or some other group to raise health awareness.

Evaluation Level

• Debate from different perspectives a conflict in a period of history that we've studied.

• Read a short story or article with a partner, and write a short essay on what you think the author's message is.

• Describe the difference between "a friend" and "a best friend." In essay form, write your descriptions and discuss why it's important to have both kind of friends.

MULTIPLE INTELLIGENCES PROJECTS FOR INTRAPERSONAL INTELLIGENCE

Knowledge Level

• Write an autobiography of your life.

• Write a series of poems titled "Who Am I?"

• Write a story that is set in or mentions places in your state that you have visited.

Comprehension Level

• Fill out the Student Inventory form and put it in your portfolio.

• Rewrite a chapter from one of the books we've read as if you were the central character and your friends were included. Show how the character could have done something differently to change the outcome of the story. Share your story with your classmates.

• Compare yourself now with a "younger you." How have you changed? How are you the same? Write a short report on your comparisons.

Application Level

• Research the animal you'd most like to be, make notes, and present your reasons to the class.

• Start a scrapbook for this year in your life.

• Create a dance that illustrates each stage of your life.

• Teach a younger class one way to resolve conflicts.

Analysis Level

- Keep a journal of your feelings and attitudes. After one month, write down how your feelings and attitudes have changed.
- Keep a diary, graph, or chart of how different activities make you feel.
- Make a musical cassette of different songs and explain to the class how each one makes you feel—for example, happy, sad, excited.
- Observe other students for three days and keep notes on how individual students react to events and social situations.
- Write an advice column for imaginary readers discussing how to handle certain problems or emotions.

Synthesis Level

- Express your moods through a series of sculptures, pictures, songs, or poems.
- Explain how different moods and emotions cause you to behave differently.
- Invent a computer program that would help students recognize how they are feeling when they are upset and advise on what to do to feel better.

Evaluation Level

- Create a Venn Diagram that compares how you are similar and different from a family member or friend. Write a paragraph about how you would like a family member or friend to be more like you and why.
- Write an essay comparing yourself to a family member. Pay close attention to how you and this person are similar and different in your emotions, opinions, and interests.
- Write a letter of recommendation for yourself.

MULTIPLE INTELLIGENCES PROJECTS FOR MATH-LOGIC INTELLIGENCE

Knowledge Level

- Make an outline of the scientific process.
- Study and make examples of different types of graphs (line, circle, pie, etc.).
- Find out all you can about the history of math and write a short report on your findings.
- Make a list of all the math terms you know.

Comprehension Level

• Research and explore algebra. What is it? What's its purpose?

• Write an experiment based on the scientific method.

• Using the entire school site, locate examples of:

    1. geometric shapes and sketch them.

    2. math being used in everyday life.

• Explain the origin of geometry and how it's used in real life.

Application Level

• Create a song or poem to teach multiplication facts.

• Make a mind bender (a complex math problem) for the class to solve.

• Using math (addition, multiplication, etc.), make up a playground game.

• Make a chart that compares the characteristics of the planets in the solar system.

• Learn how to play chess and teach it to the class.

Analysis Level

• Conduct a survey and graph the data. Write a brief paragraph about your findings.

• Create a poster or poem that uses simple terms to explain a complicated math concept. (For example, how addition is used in multiplication or how to remember the different polygons by knowing that the polygon names relate to the different number of sides.)

• Categorize objects found in the classroom and at home into geometric-shape categories. Then explain why you think these shapes are most common and why other shapes are not used as frequently in daily life.

• Make a time line showing important discoveries and changes in the history of math. Then explain why you think the discoveries were made in the order they were.

Synthesis Level

• Develop a series of lessons and games that will teach your classmates how to use the calculator.

• Use charts or cards to create a series of number sequences. Have the class find the patterns.

• Use math concepts to design and build a model of a building or a machine.

• Design a way to teach a younger child a math concept and give it a try!

• Design a way to teach geometric shapes to a blind person.

Developing Students' Multiple Intelligences • Scholastic Professional Books

Evaluation Level

- Keep a math journal in which you reflect on your strengths and weaknesses in learning math. Why do you think you are a good, average, or poor math student?
- Rank your favorite and least favorite parts of math, and explain why you like your favorite parts the best.
- Write a letter of recommendation for yourself related to your math skills.

MULTIPLE INTELLIGENCES PROJECTS FOR MUSICAL INTELLIGENCE

Knowledge Level

- Learn to play a song and perform it for the class.
- List all of the musical instruments you know by memory. Then research instruments and ask others to see if you have missed any.

Comprehension Level

- Listen to different types of music (rock, classical, jazz, etc.) and explain the differences to the class.
- Illustrate a story or poem using sound effects.
- Research a famous musician and tell the class about him or her.
- Research a unique musical instrument and tell four friends about it.

Application Level

- You are in charge of the National Musical Awards this year. Who would you choose to receive awards and why?
- Conduct a scientific experiment to test the effect of music on school performance.
- Make a musical cassette of sounds found in nature.
- Demonstrate the different types of music found in the U.S.

Analysis Level

- Bring in an example of classical music and play it for the class. Discuss the various parts of the piece to help your classmates understand that it is made up of a lot of different elements.
- Research sound waves and make a presentation to the class explaining what a sound wave is and how it affects our daily lives. Talk about how what we hear as one sound

is really a combination of a lot of different sound waves.

• Compare two different types of music using a Venn Diagram to explain the similarities and differences.

Synthesis Level

• Use songs/raps to create a language arts lesson on a particular skill (grammar, spelling, etc.).
• Create a drawing or painting for a CD cover.
• Create and write a radio program. Present it to a group of students.
• Make up a series of jump rope or ball-bouncing jingles.
• Create an original dance or piece of music to share with the class.
• Find or write a song about a science concept. Present it to the class.

Evaluation Level

• Choose a current piece of music and critique it. Write a review recommending it or discouraging classmates from listening to it.
• Make a list of your top ten favorite singers. Rank them in order of 1–10 and explain why you ranked them as you did.
• Do you feel that children who are excellent musicians should be able to perform professionally and not go to school full time? Instead, could they be taught at home and concentrate on their music? Would this hurt children in the long run? Write your thoughts.

MULTIPLE INTELLIGENCES PROJECTS FOR SPATIAL INTELLIGENCE

Knowledge Level

• Draw a series of pictures illustrating a book you are reading.
• Choose a famous painting and create your own version of it.
• Make a list of all the artists you know by memory. Then ask friends and family members to add to your list. Check the spelling of the names and share your list with the class.

Comprehension Level

• Choose an artist and write about his or her work and what makes the work unique. Share examples with the class.

Developing Students' Multiple Intelligences • Scholastic Professional Books

- Compare two artists and their styles. Make a chart showing the ways they are similar and different.
- Explain abstract art to the class in a five-minute oral report. Show examples.

Students learn geometric shapes through a spatial hands-on art project which requires them to draw, measure and cut out pieces of cloth.

Application Level

- Make up a Pictionary game using words from one of our subject areas.
- Make up a math game using tangrams.
- Use map symbols to make an accurate, professional-looking map of your neighborhood.
- Use a graphic design program on the computer to design a house or landscape a yard.
- Make a floor plan of your school.
- Make a topographic map.
- Develop a three-dimensional model of something you have learned in math.

Analysis Level

- Draw a map that features important events in history.
- Take metric measurements of various objects found in school or on the playground. Organize the data on a chart.
- Create an advertisement for a gallery that is displaying a famous artist's work.

Synthesis Level

- Create a time line describing what happens to a character or how a plot unfolds.
- Create a mural, logo, or poster reflecting a period of history.
- Create a picture collage on a science topic.
- Create a quilt pattern using geometric designs.
- Pretend you are microscopic and can travel in one of the body's systems. Write and draw a presentation about what you see.
- Design a school playground.

- Design a new park for your neighborhood. Survey neighbors and friends to see what they'd like included.

Evaluation Level

- Debate with a friend the truth of the quote, "Beauty is in the eye of the beholder." Summarize your debate in writing.
- Recommend ten pieces of art to the class. Tell why you like these pieces.
- Some companies require their employees to have photo identifications with them at all times. Do you think this is a good idea? Why or why not?

MULTIPLE INTELLIGENCES PROJECTS FOR VERBAL-LINGUISTIC INTELLIGENCE

Knowledge Level

- Write and illustrate a picture book that focuses on a specific grade level. When you are done, read your book to a younger class.
- Write a letter to a politician regarding a subject you really care about.
- Write a Multiple Intelligences Newsletter and send it home with students on Friday.
- Write a letter to someone famous.
- Use the computer's word processing program to write a story or letter.

Comprehension Level

- Write poetry! Research different types of poems and then choose a couple of them to write, publish, and share with the class.
- Read a story and make a diorama depicting your favorite scene.
- Research a famous athlete and write a report about him or her.
- Research an animal and tell the class about it.

Application Level

- Make lists of different kinds of words. Some examples: words to use instead of *said*, bold adjectives, exciting action verbs, homophones, animal types.
- Illustrate a poem using colors, textures, and so on to help the poem come alive.
- Create a memory game to help memorize facts. Memorize a list or poem and recite it for the class.
- Interview a teacher, secretary, or principal to get a different view of the school. Write

up the interview and include a biography of the person.

- Use this week's spelling words to create a cross-word puzzle.
- Make up a "code language" of your own, and write a poem or a letter in that language.
- Using songs/raps, create a lesson to teach a language arts skill (grammar, spelling, etc.).

A parent helper, who has already shared her expertise in writing with the class, helps students write stories to accompany family pictures.

Analysis Level

- Write a one- to two-page report comparing two novels.
- Write a story in which the main character uses logical reasoning to solve a problem.
- Create a time line that highlights the most important events in a book you've read.

Synthesis Level

- Write a four-scene tableau of an event in history. Perform it for the class.
- Create a mind map or graphic organizer to explain important aspects—character, plot, or setting—of a story or book you've recently read.
- Give an oral report to the class about a topic that you feel strongly about. Include visuals and an activity that will help students remember the points you made.
- Write a series of letters to a book character. Explain to him or her what you think about the story and what you like or dislike about him or her.

Evaluation Level

- Read a book all week long and keep a journal of what's happening in it and how it makes you feel.
- Recommend three books for classmates to read. Summarize each book, explaining why you recommend it.
- Compare two books with similar plots but very different stories.

CURRICULUM-BASED
MULTIPLE INTELLIGENCES PROJECT LISTS

These projects are directly related to the curriculum you're presently teaching. They give students the chance to use their stronger intelligences to learn and truly understand curriculum concepts. This learning through students' stronger intelligences should translate into higher achievement scores in academic areas.

I've had many students who show very little interest in a specific area of the curriculum until they're allowed to work independently on a project that interests them. For example, Steven was a very bright but unmotivated student who hated to write. But once he had the chance to chose a topic that interested him—the personality differences between 1980 and 1990 cartoon characters—Steven wrote a seven-page paper comparing and contrasting a myriad of different types of characters. After he read his work to the class and experienced his peers' overwhelming interest, Steven realized what he could achieve through writing and became very positive about it for the rest of the year.

The easiest way for me to organize and use curriculum-based projects is to create project lists related to curriculum areas and topics. You can either allow students to choose their projects or you can assign projects. You may want to alternate between these two options to ensure that students are working at all of Bloom's Taxonomy levels.

Following are lists of curriculum-based projects for four units—the solar system, parts of speech, spelling lists, and fractions. These lists are designed to include a variety of projects that draw on all the intelligences and cover Bloom's Taxonomy levels (noted in parentheses after each project). As you begin to develop your own lists to fit your students and curriculum, you'll find that the lists will grow and expand each time you use them.

THE SOLAR SYSTEM

After students have a foundation of knowledge about the solar system from classroom reading and discussions, the following projects can enrich and strengthen their learning.

Solar System Model. Build a three-dimensional, scale model of the solar system. *(Spatial/Math-Logic—Application/Synthesis)*

Role-Play Activity. Choose a group of classmates to participate in a role-playing activity in which you are the sun and each of the other students is a planet. Write a script with the "planets" each saying something about themselves. Perform the skit for the class with everyone

Developing Students' Multiple Intelligences • Scholastic Professional Books

standing in the correct order holding signs to identify their part.
(Verbal-Linguistic/Interpersonal/Spatial—Knowledge/Comprehension)

Solar System Tableau. Write a seven-scene tableau that includes facts and information about the solar system. Choose a group of students to practice and perform the tableau.
(Verbal-Linguistic/Bodily-Kinesthetic/Spatial/Interpersonal—Application/Synthesis)

Solar System Song. Create a song to teach younger students the order of the planets. The song should have a recurring rhythm and a chorus. Perform it for the class. Choose a primary class to perform it for.
(Music/Verbal-Linguistic—Comprehension)

Solar System Report. Write a two- to three-page report about the solar system. Include three different references and one picture.
(Verbal-Linguistic/Spatial—Application)

Imaginary Journal. Write an imaginary journal for a ten-day mission into space. You have been selected as the first student to go into space. Decide where within the solar system your mission goes, and keep a daily log explaining what you are seeing and learning. You'll need to research space missions and spacecraft before writing. Use your last entry to evaluate the entire mission. How successful was it? What would you do differently? How did it make you feel?
(Verbal-Linguistic/Intrapersonal—Synthesis/Evaluation)

Solar System Math. Make a chart or graph to show the distance of each planet from the sun. Translate the actual distance into a smaller scale and draw the solar system to this scale.
(Math-Logic/Spatial—Analysis)

Famous Astronauts Play. Research famous astronauts who have played a big role in the exploration of space. Write a short skit that tells interesting facts and information about these astronauts and their missions. Perform it for the class.
(Verbal-Linguistic/Interpersonal/Bodily-Kinesthetic—Knowledge/Analysis)

PARTS OF SPEECH

I'm always amazed at how many upper-grade students walk into my classroom without the parts of speech engraved into their memory banks. I know my colleagues were teaching these

Scholastic Professional Books • Developing Students' Multiple Intelligences

grammar lessons, yet students continue to ask, "What's an adverb?" These projects can help reinforce the parts of speech after a review lesson.

Word Hunt. Make copies of four pages of a book. Then use different-colored highlighters to identify the nouns, adjectives, verbs, adverbs, and pronouns. Put a key on the first page showing which color is used to identify which part of speech.
(Verbal-Linguistic/Spatial—Knowledge/Comprehension)

Parts of Speech Book. Write a picture book to teach younger students about one part of speech—for example, nouns, adjectives, verbs, adverbs, or pronouns. Include lots of pictures and examples for the younger kids.
(Verbal-Linguistic/Spatial—Knowledge/Comprehension)

Compound Words. Write a song that teaches students what a compound word is and gives entertaining examples of compound words. Try to find compound words that are unusual and not commonly used in speech. Write out the lyrics and share them with the class.
(Music/Interpersonal—Application/Analysis)

Word P.E. Game. Create a P.E. game that teaches the different parts of speech. Teach it to the class.
(Bodily-Kinesthetic—Verbal-Linguistic—Comprehension/Synthesis)

Word Math Game. Create a math activity for the class that requires students to use the parts of speech to solve math problems. Problems can include word problems that have students count letters or syllables, or use a part of speech to solve a mystery.
(Math-Logic/Verbal-Linguistic/ Interpersonal—Application)

Autobiography. Write the story of your life. When it's completed, count the number of nouns, adjectives, verbs, adverbs, or pronouns you used. Put the total counts on the last page.
(Verbal-Linguistic/Intrapersonal/ Math-Logic—Comprehension/Synthesis)

Page Rewrite. Rewrite a page of the book you are currently reading. Identify the parts of speech, and then substitute other words for as many words as you can. For example, the verb *run* can be changed to *sprint*. Count how many changes you were able to make.
(Verbal-Linguistic—Analysis/Evaluation)

Parts of Speech Play. Using personification, write a play about the different parts of speech. Give each part of speech a name (e.g., noun = Nancy Noun). Have each character act out the role they play in grammar.
(Verbal-Linguistic/Bodily-Kinesthetic/Interpersonal—Application/Analysis)

SPELLING LISTS

I strongly believe that students need to use words meaningfully to learn to spell them—not just memorize them for a test. But I ran out of spelling activities soon after my first year of teaching. Then I began using independent projects to reinforce spelling. Now the activities are endless, my students actually enjoy their spelling work, and their overall spelling improves. Many of these activities take very little time since the words change frequently.

Spelling Calendar. Use a sheet of white construction paper folded in half to design a calendar for this month. Choose ten words from your weekly spelling list, and use them in creating ten special days to celebrate during the month. On the calendar cover, draw a thematic picture that represents the month.
(Spatial/Math-Logic— Application/Synthesis)

Creative Writing Story. Write a story and include all your spelling words in it. Highlight each spelling word when you finish. Read the story to a group of students, asking them to write each spelling word as they hear it.
(Verbal-Linguistic/ Interpersonal— Application/Synthesis)

Spelling Word TV Ad. Use all of your spelling words to write a television commercial for a product that will help students memorize their spelling words. Tell

A student uses a quiet and comfortable space to complete her creative writing story which includes her weekly spelling words.

students how the product works, and then perform the commercial for the class.
(Verbal-Linguistic/Spatial—Synthesis/Evaluation)

Spelling Word Scrapbook. Use old newspapers and magazines to make a scrapbook for your spelling words. Find a picture that illustrates or defines each word, and paste it on one page of the scrapbook. Write the word one or more times on the page. Make a scrapbook cover and include your name as the author.
(Intrapersonal/Verbal-Linguistic—Comprehension/Analysis)

Spelling Word Rap. Make up a rap song that includes all of your spelling words. Share the song with the class.
(Musical/Verbal-Linguistic—Synthesis)

Concentration Game. Using all your spelling words, create a concentration card game. Write each word on an index card. Then make a matching card for each with a picture clue, a definition, or an idea clue on it. Have 10 students play the game one at a time to test it. Make any necessary changes based on their confusion or suggestions.
(Bodily-Kinesthetic/Spatial/Interpersonal—Application/Synthesis/Evaluation)

Spelling Word Classification. Group all of your spelling words using your own classification system. Include a minimum of three words in each group. Write a sentence under each group explaining why you created each one.
(Math-Logic/Verbal-Linguistic—Analysis/Evaluation)

FRACTIONS

Some students experience a great deal of difficulty and frustration with the abstract concept of fractions. I've used the following projects to reduce the fear of fractions and to help students understand what a fraction is.

Fraction Pizza. Create a "fraction" pizza on a sheet of white construction paper. First, draw a large "pizza" circle and put a specific number of "slices" on it. Then use different-colored pens or crayons to add toppings. Somewhere in each slice, write a fraction that reflects how much of the entire pizza that slice represents. For example, if you cut the pizza into 12 slices, each slice would be 1/12 of the entire pizza.
(Math-Logic/Spatial—Analysis)

Fraction Order. Order the following fractions from largest to smallest: 1/10, 2/8, 3/4, 1/15, 7/8, and 5/12. Underneath each fraction, draw a picture to represent it.
(Math-Logic/Spatial—Analysis/Evaluation)

Fraction Story. Write a story about a fractional family. For example, the "Fourth" family has four members: 1/4, 2/4, 3/4, and 4/4. Give each member of the family a unique personality relating to its fraction.
(Math-Logic/Verbal-Linguistic—Analysis)

Fraction Song. Make up a song to help students learn about fractions. You might want to use a familiar melody. Be sure the lyrics help students understand that fractions are used to break down a "whole."
(Musical/Math-Logic/Verbal-Linguistic—Application/Analysis)

Fraction P.E. Game. Redesign a game we already play to include fractions. For example, in softball, every time a player scores, his team could score 2/3 of a point instead of one point.
(Bodily-Kinesthetic/Interpersonal—Knowledge/Synthesis)

The How-To Fraction Book. What problems did you have in learning fractions? Write a how-to book to help students with one of these problems. Include pictures, written explanations, and tips from your own experience.
(Math-Logic/Verbal-Linguistic/Spatial/Intrapersonal—Comprehension/Analysis/Evaluation)

Fraction Skit. Write and perform a short skit that teaches students how to reduce fractions. You may want to use props to show that certain fractions are equal even if they look different.
(Verbal-Linguistic/Interpersonal/Math-Logic—Comprehension/Analysis/Evaluation)

THEMATIC-BASED MULTIPLE INTELLIGENCES PROJECTS

Research has shown that the brain seeks patterns to make sense of information. And I've learned that my students can and need to find patterns in learning. They learn better if they can be shown that pieces of information are related to—and integrated with—other pieces of information. For example, you provide students with a pattern when in teaching them about governments you start with the local city government and move through the continuum of governments (state, federal, international). You can also teach multiplication using the natural patterns in the multiplication table. Most teachers have students start with the zeros, move to the ones, and so on. This way, students can detect the inherent pattern in multiplication and memorize their tables more quickly. Many times I've overheard students figure out a multiplication problem by reasoning. For example, "five times seven is . . . let's see, five times six is thirty so five times seven is thirty five." The students learn, and continue to learn, through mastering patterns.

Along with its pattern-seeking abilities, the brain searches for meaningful and relevant information. I use themes throughout the year to tie curriculum areas and activities together under a larger umbrella and to help students connect what they are learning and to realize that knowledge and skills are related. Thematic-based, multiple-intelligences, independent projects tied directly to these themes provide valuable opportunities for students to review, expand, and enrich what they are learning.

I have found that the easiest way to organize and use thematic-based projects is to create project lists related to the theme. You can either have students choose their project or assign each student a project. You may want to alternate between these two options to be sure that students are working in all of Bloom's Taxonomy levels.

Following are examples of thematic-based independent projects. As you begin to develop your own lists to suit your own students and your own themes, you'll find that they'll grow and expand each time you use them. These lists are designed to include a variety of projects that cover the intelligences and Bloom's Taxonomy. (The intelligences and the Bloom's Taxonomy levels used in each project are shown in parenthesis.)

FAIRY TALES THEME

Fairy Tale Rating. Read four fairy tales of your choice. Rate them in order of your most-to-least favorite and explain why you rated them as you did. Using your favorite fairy tale, write a short review explaining why everyone should read it.
(Verbal-Linguistic/Math-Logic/Intrapersonal—Analysis/Evaluation)

Fairy Tale Puppet Show. Create a puppet show to retell your favorite fairy tale to the class. Change one thing about the story and see if the class can guess the change.
(Verbal-Linguistic/Bodily-Kinesthetic/Interpersonal—Knowledge/Application)

Developing Students' Multiple Intelligences • Scholastic Professional Books

Fairy Tale Journal. Pretend you have been put into one of the fairy tales, and in journal form discuss the events and characters you meet. Discuss what you like and dislike about the characters. Include at least eight entries.
(Intrapersonal/Verbal-Linguistic—Synthesis/Evaluation)

Fairy Tale Logic. Choose a song that you think tells a story similar to one of the fairy tales you've read, and then write a short essay explaining why you chose this song and why it relates to your fairy tale.
(Math-Logic/Verbal-Linguistic/Musical—Analysis/Evaluation)

Fairy Tale Music. Compose a song that tells the story of one of the fairy tales. Perform it for a group of students, and have them guess which fairy tale your song represents.
(Musical/Interpersonal—Application/Synthesis)

Fairy Tale Picture Book. Create a picture book for your favorite fairy tale. Read it to another class.
(Spatial/Interpersonal—Knowledge/Comprehension)

Fairy Tale Day. Plan a Fairy Tale Day for the class, including activities for the entire day. This may include dressing up as your favorite character, eating fairy tale foods, playing games, and reading fairy tales.
(Interpersonal/Math-Logic—Application/Synthesis)

Fairy Tale Rewrite. Rewrite a fairy tale from the perspective of one of the minor characters in the story. To see an example and get some ideas, read *The True Story of the Three Little Pigs* by Jon Scieszka. Read your story to the class.
(Verbal-Linguistic/Intrapersonal—Comprehension/Analysis)

Fairy Tale Game. Create a board game with a fairy tale theme. Include all of the main parts of the story in the game. Let students play the game and give you feedback. Make any changes that would make it more fun to play.
(Math-Logic/Spatial/Interpersonal—Application/Evaluation)

Scholastic Professional Books • Developing Students' Multiple Intelligences

TIME THEME

Sundial. Construct a sundial. Explain to the class how sundials were used, and give them a brief history of the sundial.
(Spatial/Bodily-Kinesthetic—Application/Synthesis)

Dance. Learn a dance such as the Waltz or the Swing that were popular in the past and are still enjoyed. Demonstrate the dance for the class, and tell them about the history of the dance.
(Bodily-Kinesthetic/Interpersonal/Verbal Linguistic—Knowledge/Synthesis)

Baby Research. Talk to your parents and grandparents about what you were like as a baby. Look through your baby book if your parents made one. Write a brief report about your babyhood and how it made you feel to learn about yourself during that time.
(Verbal-Linguistic/Intrapersonal—Knowledge/Application/Evaluation)

Time Line. Make a time line for a period of history that we've recently studied, marking the important and interesting events. Add pictures and colors to make it more interesting.
(Spatial/Math-Logic—Analysis)

Family Scrapbook. Research your family history and create a family tree. See how far back you can trace your family members and where they were from. Use the family tree to start your scrapbook. Add funny stories or interesting facts about family members as well as pictures, letters, and drawings.
(Intrapersonal/Interpersonal/Spatial/Verbal-Linguistic—Application/Synthesis)

Music Feelings. Listen to several pieces of music that have different rhythms and speeds. Write a short paper on how slow music makes you feel compared to fast music. Make sure to identify the songs and their singers or composers.
(Musical/Intrapersonal—Analysis/Evaluation)

Be on Time! Prepare a five-minute oral report on the importance of being on time. Give students a list of reasons why you feel being on time is important.
(Verbal-Linguistic/Interpersonal—Analysis/Evaluation)

Seasonal Fashions. Design a report to show how the seasons influence the clothes we

Developing Students' Multiple Intelligences • Scholastic Professional Books

wear, the food we eat, and the games we play. Use drawings and pictures from magazines to make your report come alive.

(Spatial/Verbal-Linguistic/Interpersonal—Knowledge/Analysis)

Calendar Detective. Research how our calendar was developed. Then tell the class what you found, giving them a brief history of the calendar.

(Verbal-Linguistic/ Math-Logic/Interpersonal—Comprehension/Analysis)

RESOURCE-BASED MULTIPLE INTELLIGENCES PROJECTS

For the past few years, I've heard the term Information Age used frequently. But it wasn't until I began working on this book that I really learned what it meant. I learned that in 1954, information doubled every 20 years; in 1996 it doubles every 30–36 months. By the year 2000, it will double every 12–18 months. The statistics are jarring. The amount of information available to me on the World Wide Web, in libraries, on television, and in magazines and newspapers is almost overwhelming. I figured that if it's overwhelming for me, it must be simply staggering for my students. It's essential that they learn how to find, analyze, and use the information at their fingertips to meet the challenge of living in the Information Age. Resource-based projects focus on helping students make sense of the incredible amount of information available to them.

What They Need to Know

According to the American Library Association (ALA), "people need more than just a knowledge base. They also need techniques for exploring it, connecting it to other knowledge bases, and making practical use of it." The American Library Association Presidential Committee on Information Literacy: Final Report defines Information Literacy as being able to:

1. know when there is a need for information.
2. identify information needed to address a given problem or issue.
3. find needed information.
4. evaluate the information.
5. organize the information.
6. use the information effectively to address the problem or issue at hand.

Resource-based projects help students explore learning and become information literate. They offer common-sense approaches to learning that—coupled with the different intelligences—become a powerful and meaningful learning opportunity. They provide repeated experiences and opportunities for students to work with the same real-world information resources and technologies that will bombard them throughout their lives. The multiple intelligences help provide a natural context within which my students can store and organize information as they make their way toward becoming information literate.

Reports—A New View

I focus resource-based projects around reports. For years when I assigned reports, my students would moan and groan all the way to the library. There they would find books, many of which were outdated, and begin copying information and facts word for word. Students would continually ask, "Mrs. Nelson, can you help me find a book?" Once most of the students had some type of book, I would collapse in a heap and promise myself not to assign a report for a long time to come. Students would then attempt to filter through the information, transcribe it into their own words, and produce a report. The whole process was more of a nuisance than a real learning experience.

It was after one of these days in the library that I came to a startling conclusion: my students lacked skills in finding information and analyzing it for their reports. My students were information illiterate! I decided then and there to teach students to gather information from many sources, read for information, analyze it thoroughly, and reinvent in creating their own work. I realized that I could use the multiple intelligences to bring order into the chaotic world of information and to help students learn that information comes in many forms.

Resource-based projects are long-term projects for which students gather information and research a specific topic. These topics can be directly related to the curriculum or current classroom theme. The variety of topics my students have researched include the Civil War, ancient China, famous scientists, Sir Isaac Newton, presidents, Louisa May Alcott, writing genres, the history of computers, geometry, and how a town is developed.

To get students started on the road of information-gathering using the eight intelligences, give students a copy of the Multiple Intelligences Information-Gathering Suggestions worksheet on the following page. This sheet will help remind students that information is accessible from many kinds of sources. It will spur students' prior knowledge of the multiple intelligences as well as identify the information they need to gather.

Developing Students' Multiple Intelligences • Scholastic Professional Books

Multiple Intelligences
Information-Gathering Suggestions

1. INTRAPERSONAL:

What do I already know about the topic? How do I know this information is correct? Where did I learn this information? Do I already have strong opinions and feelings about this topic?

2. INTERPERSONAL:

What do people around me know about the topic—my parents, grandparents, sister, brother, aunt, uncle, friends? Do I trust that their information is correct? Did I ask how they learned this information?

3. VERBAL-LINGUISTIC:

What do books and magazines tell me about the topic? Is there information I can get from the computer and Internet? Have I tried the school library and the public library? Do my parents have any books at home that can help?

4. MATH-LOGIC:

What information can I find about the economy or costs of the topic? Is there any financial information I can find? Is there any information about distances, geography, and charts I can use? Can I use technology tools to gather data?

5. MUSICAL:

Is there any music that teaches me about the topic? Are there any songs or musical history that relates to the topic? Are there videos that can provide me with information?

6. BODILY-KINESTHETIC:

Are there dances that relate to the topic? Are there plays or skits written about the topic that will give me information? Are there sports played that relate to the topic?

7. SPATIAL:

Are there photographs I can use in my report? Can I draw a map or picture about what I've learned? Are there charts or graphs that can give me valuable information?

8. NATURALIST:

Do nature and wildlife relate to my topic? If so, why are they important? Do plants and animals have a role in something that happened?

STUDENT-CHOICE MULTIPLE INTELLIGENCES PROJECTS

I've found that certain students who don't respond positively to school and/or homework come alive when they have a voice in their own learning. So I let students choose or design their own multiple intelligences projects whenever the curriculum and time allow. These student-choice projects are particularly effective at those times of the year—usually around grading periods—when I need time to meet with students individually to set goals and talk to them about their progress. Working on their own projects, students are self-motivated and work well independently. And I have the time I need for individual conferences. I've had students do their most advanced and challenging work when they are given the power of choice.

To help students get started on choosing a project, I provide them with a general direction. For example, I tell them that their project should be based on one of the multiple intelligences categories or related to the theme we're involved with in class. Then I step back and turn the students loose to design or choose their own projects. Many students are motivated to design projects that excite them. Others immediately turn to the projects lists I've prepared. Here are four rules I discuss with the class before they start:

1. Choose a project topic that you truly want to learn more about, experiment with, or research.

2. Don't copy your friend's project ideas. Be original!

3. Don't choose a project that is too easy for you. I know you well and I'll be the first to tell you it's too easy.

4. Plan for a project you can complete within one to three weeks.

After students have decided on their project, I require them to submit a project plan that tells me exactly what they'll be doing and describes an overall plan of action. I use the Project Sheet: Presenting What I've Learned (see next page) to give students starting points for planning their project. Once I have their plans, I meet with students individually to clear up any questions or concerns I may have. I also keep a weekly chart for each student showing project due dates so I can keep track of how they're doing. Added to the students' portfolios, these charts provide a running record of the various types of projects they've completed.

Project Sheet: Presenting What I've Learned
One strategy in student-choice projects is to use the Project Sheet: Presenting What I've Learned worksheet. This worksheet can help students choose a project.

Developing Students' Multiple Intelligences • Scholastic Professional Books

Project Sheet:
Presenting What I've Learned

I am choosing the following project to show that I have learned a lot about

_____ .

_____ Write a report

_____ Build a three-dimensional model

_____ Present an oral report to the class

_____ Develop a musical piece to explain it to the class

_____ Make up a dance that represents what I have learned

_____ Write and perform a short skit

_____ Design a chart, graph, or mind map

_____ Engage in a debate or discussion with another student and then
write down the main ideas of the conversation

_____ Keep a daily journal about this subject

_____ Compile a scrapbook

_____ Make an art project and explain the project in writing

_____ Produce a videotape segment

_____ Research the subject and write the information down

_____ Set up an experiment and show/explain it to the class

_____ Teach a small group of my classmates about the information

_____ Develop a project not listed above:

On the back of this page is a brief description of what I intend to do.

_____   _____
Signature of Student   Date

_____   _____
Signature of Teacher   Date

_____   _____
Signature of Parent   Date

Classroom Project Sheet

Student Name	Date	Due Date	Project	Intelligences/ Bloom's Taxonomy
Joe	3/4/97	4/6/97	Writing play using Greek gods intermingling with Roman gods. Act out.	Linguistic/ Interpersonal— Analysis/Synthesis
Carol	3/4/97	4/6/97	Solar system model with written explanation of facts.	Spatial/Math-Logic/ Verbal-Linguistic— Knowledge/Application
Kim	3/5/97	4/8/97	Small-group debate regarding Civil War events with a role-play as final activity.	Interpersonal/Verbal-Linguistic/Visual-Spatial-Knowledge/ Analysis/Synthesis
Juan	3/6/97	4/10/97	Imaginary journal studying different bird species in the Amazon River area.	Naturalist/Verbal-Linguistic/Interpersonal-Application/ Comprehension
Karen	3/6/97	4/12/97	P.E. game using parts of speech and word patterns. Written rules and information.	Bodily-Kinesthetic/ Verbal-Linguistic/Inter-personal-Application/ Comprehension
Lougene	3/8/97	4/13/97	Venn diagram comparing self with family and friends.	Math-Logic/Interpersonal/ Intrapersonal-Analysis/Evaluation
Ronda	3/10/97	4/10/97	Creating a song to teach primary students addition and subtraction. Will teach small group in Mrs. Anderson's class.	Musical/Math-Interpersonal-Knowledge/Synthesis

Multiple Intelligences Project Assessment Form

Student Name _____ Grade _____

Project Title/Description _____

Curriculum Area _____ Intelligence(s) Focus _____

Project Start Date _____ Project Complete Date _____

1. How well does the project relate to the subject?	1	2	3	4	5	NA
2. Quality of work: neatness, presentation, etc.	1	2	3	4	5	NA
3. How much time and effort went into project?	1	2	3	4	5	NA
4. How well did student use resources/research?	1	2	3	4	5	NA
5. Was the student aware of what intelligence(s) s/he was working in to complete project?	1	2	3	4	5	NA
6. Does the project demonstrate progress beyond previous projects?	1	2	3	4	5	NA
7. Did the student collaborate well with others to get help, receive feedback, or assess work?	1	2	3	4	5	NA
8. How original and creative is the project?	1	2	3	4	5	NA
9. How accurately did student assess the project?	1	2	3	4	5	NA
10. How well did the student present the project to the class?	1	2	3	4	5	NA

Additional Comments:

Total Points: _____ out of a possible _____ points. Final Grade/Score: _____

Individual Projects...
What Do I Think?

1. I usually have students work on independent projects in the following ways:

2. From my perspective, the benefits of having students work on independent projects are:

3. The most difficult thing about assigning independent projects is:

4. The projects I assign tend to require students to use the following intelligences most:

5. The projects I assign tend to require students to use the following intelligences least:

6. I can use my dominant intelligences to strengthen my students' independent projects and/or project time in the following ways:

Chapter 5

Teaching Literacy Skills Using Multiple Intelligences Strategies

For many years, I required students to only use their verbal-linguistic intelligence to learn reading, writing, and speaking skills. This seemed obvious, and it worked just fine for the students who walked into my classroom with a natural verbal-linguistic strength. But after working with the MI theory, I realized that many of my students need to use their particular intelligence strengths to master the worlds of sounds, words, and language acquisition.

For example, a few years ago, I had a sixth-grade student who was reading at a second-grade level. She had a wonderful sight vocabulary and was one of the strongest oral readers in my class. Yet she did not understand one word she read. Her self-esteem was low, and she constantly hung her head when I asked questions about a literature selection. Luckily, by the time she came to my class, I was using multiple intelligences techniques and was able to assess her in terms of intelligence strengths. I found that her natural intelligence strengths were spatial and bodily-kinesthetic. Instead of focusing only on the verbal-linguistic methods—methods that had failed her in the past—I was able to use these to help her.

Although she could read words easily, she didn't know the meanings of many common words used often in literature. So developing her vocabulary was my starting point in devising activities that took advantage of her strengths. For months I had her write words; make flash cards that included the word, its meaning, and a picture; act out meanings; and help younger students with their vocabulary activities. Once her vocabulary began to increase, we began to read easier books, making mind maps and graphic organizers of the events in the story. Several of my other students also benefited from these lessons. Within a few months, this sixth grader's comprehension had jumped from the second- to the fourth-grade level and she was gaining confidence in her reading abilities.

Because of this young girl and many others like her, I now provide avenues for students to master reading, writing, and learning the English language using more than just the verbal-linguistic intelligence. The following lists provide simple activities and strategies to help students learn to read, appreciate literature, and enjoy the world of words using multiple intelligences strategies as guides. Many of these strategies can serve as a foundation for second-language learners to use their natural knowledge and skills. For the majority of my students, primary- and second-language learners, they have opened doors and windows to the world of language.

PRIMARY-GRADE MULTIPLE INTELLIGENCES READING STRATEGIES

BODY-SMART METHODS
- Have students write before reading.
- Make letters with clay, paint, in sand or flour, and with the typewriter and word processor.
- Use hand movements and body formations to show letters.
- Trace letters on students' palms, and help students trace sandpaper letters.
- Use jump rope chants with letters for exercise breaks.

- Play Simon Says with commands such as "Simon says, write a *B* in the air."
- Have students touch once under each word (not syllable) as they read.
- Have students practice emergent reading skills by holding a book and turning pages left-to-right as they "read" the pages.
- Write letters and words in the air.
- Write key words on sheets of construction paper, and place these on the ground in the shape of a hopscotch game. Have students practice saying and spelling words as they play the game. (Alternative: Write the words on a playground hopscotch game with chalk.)

MUSIC-SMART METHODS
- Use simple poems and rhythmic, repetitive stories.
- Use lyrics to simple songs to practice letters and reading.
- Sing the sounds.
- Use alphabet songs.
- Use tongue twisters to practice and isolate specific sounds.
- Have students sing the words in the book.

PICTURE-SMART METHODS
- Have students use a ruler or strip of paper to underline what they're reading.
- Make pictures out of letters or groups of letters
- Use different colors on bulletin boards to represent specific sounds.
- Draw "word pictures" to show the meaning of the words. For example, *tall* would be written with tall letters, and *rain* would be written with drops around it.
- Have students circle the same word on each page.
- Use books that are appropriate to students' age, interest, and conceptual ability.
- Have students draw a picture to represent a word and write the word inside the picture.
- Use Big Books (oversized story books). Have the class use construction paper to make one of their own.

NUMBER-SMART METHODS
- Write sight words, numbered from 1–25, on a poster board. When students ask how to spell a word on the list, refer them to the appropriate number on the poster.
- Use word patterns and regularities and phonics rules.
- Make dice with letters instead of dots on them.

- Use a flannel board with cloth letters or a metal board with magnetic letters. Show students how new words are formed by changing one letter (fine, dine, line).
- Locate letters numerically in the alphabet by creating a poster that shows letters ordered that way (A=1, B=2, etc.).

WORD-SMART METHODS

- Provide language experiences by writing down stories as children tell them to you.
- Use word flash cards.
- Teach pre-reading skills—holding books, turning pages, and reading from left to right.
- Use worksheets and tracing activities.
- Have students learn word families—words that are phonetically alike or sound similar.
- Use echo reading. Students repeat what is read by the primary reader.
- Read Big Books to the class.
- Reread stories.

PEOPLE-SMART METHODS

- Make reading a social event in the classroom.
- Have students take turns reading letters, words, sentences, etc.
- Read aloud together.
- Have student partners read a book together.
- Have students teach younger children the alphabet and sight words.
- Have reading parties at which students read individually and in small groups and listen to guest readers who are visiting the class.
- Use choral reading, with students reading a passage together.

SELF-SMART METHODS

- Provide a quiet, cozy reading corner.
- Give students opportunities to read silently.
- Provide books that have a high-interest value.
- Keep special "Book-Favorites" lists on a bulletin board where students can write their "All-Time Favorites."
- Have students practice reading aloud to a stuffed animal.
- Have students listen to a tape-recorded story and follow along in the book.

UPPER-GRADE MULTIPLE INTELLIGENCES READING STRATEGIES

BODILY-KINESTHETIC INTELLIGENCE

- Have students act out/role-play the story.
- Have students create tableaus explaining the main plot.
- Have students track their reading with their finger or a bookmark.
- Have students physically embody different linguistic concepts. For example, they can act out their spelling and vocabulary words.
- Have students impersonate a character in the story to explain how she or he is feeling.

Students use the tools of technology to complete a research assignment and publish a final product which will be graded on content and on how well they used technology in their project.

SPATIAL INTELLIGENCE

- Have students use graphic organizers (Venn diagrams, flow charts, graphs, mind maps).
- Have students show their comprehension through various art forms.
- Have students predict the next chapter and picture it in their minds.
- Have students build a scene for the setting of a story.
- Have students role-play having imaginary conversations with book characters.
- Have students keep a long-term collage that they add to as the story progresses.
- Have students keep an art journal, in which they draw scenes from the story as they read it.
- Have students create posters and brochures to explain phonetic rules, the writing process, and grammar rules.

- Have students create
  visual flash cards—
  with the word on one
  side and a picture of it
  on the other—of words
  they are learning.

MUSICAL INTELLIGENCE

- Play music that has a
  tone that relates to a
  story you've just read
  to the class.
- Have students find
  music that depicts the
  tone of the story.
- Put the story to music
  and sing or play it.
- Have students associ-
  ate various kinds of music and rhythm with different characters, parts of the story,
  parts of the writing process, phonetic rules, and so on.
- Use song lyrics to teach phonetic rules or how to use words.
- Have students sing the words in the book.
- Use poetry to teach rhyming and repeated words.

This student reviews his alphabet in a visual-spatial way by completing a puzzle.

VERBAL-LINGUISTIC INTELLIGENCE

- Read stories together and ask comprehension and higher-level thinking questions.
- Use worksheets to provide repetitive practice.
- Have students write a summary of a story.
- Have students debate the decisions characters made during the story.
- Have students read aloud into a tape recorder, and then play back the tape and assess
  their oral reading skills.
- Have students take home and listen to a book tape-recorded by a classmate.
- Have students retell the story in their own words.
- Have students predict what will happen as the story progresses.
- Model oral reading skills to students. Talk to them about reading fluency, embellish-

ment, and varied intonations. Have them identify when you are using these skills.

- Reread books or parts of a book for guided reading practice.
- Use dialogue reading. Assign students a specific book character's dialogue to read aloud.
- Use Reader's Theater. Assign students parts of the script to read aloud.

MATHEMATICAL-LOGICAL INTELLIGENCE

- Ask students questions in the form of syllogisms: "If _____ , then _____."
- Use similarities and comparisons between characters or stories to demonstrate comprehension.
- Have students make a time line to show the order of events.
- Have students create character charts outlining the story characters' important characteristics.
- Present words in list form, showing similarities and differences between word families. For example, act, react, and deactivate would be listed together.
- Use Venn diagrams to show similarities and differences.
- Use the pretest-study-test sequence.

INTERPERSONAL INTELLIGENCE

- Have students read with partners and discuss the story events.
- Use reading groups.
- Have students read books aloud to a partner.
- Designate Reading Days when students read and are read to all day.
- Have students help younger students with their reading.
- Have Mock Talk Show Days with characters from the story, and have them explain what is happening in the story.
- Use Oral-Reading Partner Tutoring. Have students read aloud to another student. The listening student assesses the oral reading and offers advice. The student tries again with the advice in mind. Students alternate reading aloud.
- Use Popcorn Reading. The whole class reads a literature selection aloud. One student reads and then calls on another student to continue reading.
- Use choral reading. Students read passages together.
- Have students form Literature Circles, in which groups of students read and discuss passages from literature selections they're reading independently. Each student contributes thoughts about the characters, the author, and any other aspect of the selection. Students discuss how they like the story, theme, or conflict.
- Use Jigsaw Reading in which a group of students reads a literature selection together.

Then each student becomes an expert on one section and is responsible for teaching the other students about that section.

INTRAPERSONAL INTELLIGENCE
- Designate Reading Nooks in the classroom that are private and comfortable.
- Have students choose a way to show that they understand the story.
- Provide time for silent reading.
- Have students keep a Word Log or Book Log to show the words they are learning and the books they are reading.
- Have students write a summary of a story they read, describing their favorite parts and explaining why they like those parts.
- Have students use multimodality techniques to learn spelling and vocabulary independently.
- Have students assess their own reading strengths and areas of improvement.
- Have students listen to a tape-recorded story and follow along in the book.

MULTIPLE INTELLIGENCES LITERATURE

You can using literature to awaken and nurture all your students' intelligences in a natural way. No matter what grade I'm teaching, I try to read picture books to students regularly. To assist them in their own projects, I feel it's important for my upper-grade students to "see" literature as well as become familiar with the style and length of picture books.

I began the following lists of books that enrich the various intelligences several years ago and have had teachers in all grades add to them. I use them to supplement my teaching strengths and weaknesses. One look at my plan book showed me that I was rarely having students use their musical or visual-spatial intelligences—mainly because these are my two weaker areas. So I began to broaden my teaching by reading students books from those two lists. As my teaching became more balanced, I branched out to use all of the lists on a regular basis.

Many more books could be added to these lists, and many that are listed under one intelligence truly address several intelligences. I haven't put these books in grade-level categories because I believe that books at all grade levels can be used to teach a theme or stir a discussion. This is a starting point to help you ensure that your classroom offers students a broad range of literature and reading material. Happy reading!

MATH-LOGIC INTELLIGENCE LITERATURE

Books and literature that bring students into the world of math and logic take on a special importance. Especially significant for those students who view math right up there with visits to the orthodontist, they provide a different medium to experience math and logic. Math-logic books include those with predictable stories, those with patterns and replication, and those that use pictures and graphics to present math and science. The following list will start you out on this journey:

Albert Einstein, Ibi Lepscky. Barron's, 1992.*

Anno's Counting Book, Mitsumasa Anno, HarperCollins, 1992.*

Anno's Counting House, Mitsumasa Anno, Philomel, 1982.*

As the Crow Flies: A First Book of Maps, Gail Hartman, Bradbury Press, 1991.

Black Pioneers of Science and Invention, Louis Haber. Harcourt Brace Jovanovich, 1992.

Count Your Way Through Africa, Jim Haskins. Carolrhoda Books, 1992.*

Count Your Way Through China, Jim Haskins. Carolrhoda Books, 1987.*

Count Your Way Through Italy, Jim Haskins. Carolrhoda Books, 1986.*

Domino Addition, Lynette Long. Charlesbridge, 1996.*

Eating Fractions, Bruce McMillan. Scholastic Inc., 1991.*

The Eleventh Hour, Graeme Base. Harry N. Abrams, Inc. 1989.*

Grandfather Tang's Story, Ann Tompert. Crown Publishers, 1990.

How Many Snails? Paul Giganti, Jr. Greenwillow Books, 1988. *

How Much Is a Million?, David M. Schwarz. Lothrop, Lee & Shepard Books, 1985.*

The Icky Bug Counting Book, Jerry Pallotta. Charlesbridge, 1992.*

If You Give a Mouse a Cookie, Laura Numeroff. HarperFestival, 1992.*

Is There Room on the Bus? Helen Piers and Hannalt Giffard. Simon and Schuster Books for Young Readers, 1996.*

Knots on a Counting Rope, Bill Martin Jr. and John Archambault. Henry Holt and Co., 1987.

Left and Right, Joanne Oppenheim. Harcourt Brace Jovanovich, 1989.*

Majo Means One, Muriel Feelings. Dial Books for Young Readers, 1976.*

Math Curse, Jon Scieszka and Lane Smith. Viking, 1995.*

The asterisks identify the picture books on the lists.

Million Fish… More or Less, Patricia McKissack. Alfred A. Knopf, 1996.*

Numbears, Kathleen Hague. Henry Holt and Co., 1986.*

Numblers, Suse MacDonald. Dial Books for Young Readers, 1988.*

One Cow Coughs: A Counting Book for the Sick and Miserable, Christine Loomis. Ticknor and Fields Books for Young Readers, 1994.*

One Gorilla, Atsuko Morozumi. Farrar, Straus and Giroux, 1990.*

101 Dalmations: A Counting Book, Fran Manushkin. Disney Press, 1991.*

One Hundred Angry Ants, Elinor Pinczes. Houghton Mifflin, 1993.*

One Potato, Diana Pmeroy. Harcourt Brace and Co., 1996.*

One Smiling Grandma, Ann Marie Linden. Dial Books for Young Readers, 1992.*

Reading the Numbers, Mary Blocksma. Penguin Books, 1989.

School Bus, Donald Crews. Mulberry Books, 1993.*

The Secret Birthday Message, Eric Carle. Harper Trophy, 1986.*

Shapes, Shapes, Shapes, Tana Hoban. Greenwillow Books, 1986.*

Sheep in Wolve's Clothing, Satoshi Kitamura. Farrar, Straus and Giroux. 1995.*

Sideways Arithmetic from Wayside School, Louis Sachar. Scholastic Inc., 1989.

Teddy Bears Go Shopping, Susanna Gretz. Puffin Books, 1983.*

Ten Bears in My Bed, Stan Mack. Pantheon, 1974.*

10 Black Dots, Donald Crew. Greenwillow Books, 1986.*

Ten Little Mice, Joyce Dunbar. Harcourt Brace Jovanovich, 1990.*

Ten, Nine, Eight, Molly Bang. Scholastic Inc., 1983.*

Topsy-Turviews, Mitsumasa Anno. Walker/Weatherhill, 1970.*

26 Letters and 99 Cents, Tana Hoban. Morrow, 1995.

12 Ways to Get 11, Eve Merriam and Bernie Karlin. Simon and Schuster Books for Young Readers, 1993.*

Two Is for Dancing, Wookleigh Hubbard. Chronicle Books, 1991.*

Two Ways to Count to Ten, Dee Ruby. Henry Holt and Co., 1990.*

What Comes in 2's, 3's and 4's?, Susanne Aker. Simon and Schuster, Books for Young Readers, 1990.*

When Sheep Cannot Sleep, Satoshi Kitamura. Farrar, Straus and Giroux, 1986.*

You Made a Million, David M. Schwarz. Lothrop, Lee & Shepard Books, 1989.*

17 Kings and 42 Elephants, Margaret Mahy. Dial Books for Young Readers, 1990.*

VERBAL-LINGUISTIC INTELLIGENCE LITERATURE

With the books in this area I hope to increase students' awareness of the many ways language is used. I want them to glimpse the fun of using language for entertainment and humor and inspire them to go beyond the writing-to-complete-an-assignment mentality. Frequently I read a picture book to students before a grammar or language lesson to increase their motivation in these areas. The literature in this category includes books that have fun with words, books on tape, magazines, and word searches and crossword puzzle books.

A Cache of Jewels, Ruth Heller. Grosset and Dunlap, 1987.*

The Alphabet Tree, Leo Lionni. A Trumpet Club Special Edition, 1968.*

American Tall Tales, Mara Pope Osborne. Scholastic Inc., 1991.

Andy, Tomie dePaola. Prentice-Hall, 1973.*

Animalia, Graeme Base. Harry Abrams Inc., 1986.*

Anno's Counting House, Mitsumasa Anno. Philomel, 1982.*

The Beanstalk Incident, Jim Paulson. Carol Publishing Group, 1990.*

Bennet Cerf's Book of Animal Riddles, Bennett Cerf. Random, 1959.*

The Desert Is Theirs, Byrd Baylor. Aladdin, 1987.*

Dinner at Aunt Connie's House, Faith Ringgold. Hyperion Books for Children, 1993.*

The Doorbell Rang, Pat Hutchins. Greenwillow Books, 1986.*

The Dove Dove: Funny Homograph Riddles, Marvin Terban. Houghton Mifflin, 1988.

Fortunately, Rely Charlie. Four Winds, 1980.*

The Handmade Alphabet, Laura Rankin. Dial Books, 1991.*

How a Book Is Made, Alibi. Cromwell, 1986.*

The Icky Bug Alphabet Book, Jerry Pallotta. Children's Press, 1991.*

I Hate English, Ellen Levinc. Scholastic, 1989.*

Imagine, Alison Lester. Houghton Mifflin, 1990.*

Jake Baked the Cake, B. G. Hennessy. Viking Penguin, 1990.*

Jolly Postman, Janet P. and Allan Ahlberg. Little, Brown and Co., 1986.*

Just So Stories, Rudyard Kipling. Doubleday, 1972.

Kites Sail High, Ruth Heller. Grosset and Dunlap, 1988.*

Koko's Kitten, Francine Patterson. Scholastic Inc., 1985.*

Koko's Story, Francine Patterson. Scholastic Inc., 1987.*

Little Red Hen, Paul Galdone. Clarion Books, 1973.*

Mad as a Wet Hen, Marvis Terban. Clarion Books, 1987.

Max Makes a Million, Maria Kalman. Viking Penguin, 1990.*

Merry-Go-Round, A Book About Nouns, Ruth Heller. Putnam, 1990.*

Moja Means One, Muriel Feelings. Dial Publishing, 1971.*

Monika Beisner's Book of Riddles, Monika Beisner. Farrar, Straus and Giroux, 1983.*

My Mom Can't Read, Muriel Stanek. Albert Whitman & Co., 1986.*

My Mother Never Listens to Me, Marjorie Weinman Sharmat. Albert Whitman & Co., 1984.*

Nicholas Cricket, Joyce Maxner. Harper & Row, 1989.*

One Sun: A Book of Terse Verse, Bruce McMillan. Holiday House, 1990.*

The Pagemaster, David Kirschner and Ernie Contreras. Turner Publishing, Inc., 1993.*

Q Is for Duck, Mary Elting and Michael Folson. Clarion Books, 1980.*

Sad Underwear and Other Complications, Judith Viorst. Atheneum Books for Young Readers, 1995. (poetry)

The Signmaker's Assistant, Ted Arnold. Dial Books, 1992.*

The Story of Jumping Mouse, John Steptoe. Lothrop, Lee and Shepard Books, 1984.*

The Story Snail, Anne Rockwell. Macmillan, 1974.*

Sweet Clara and the Freedom Quilt, Deborah Hopkinson. Alfred A. Knopf, 1993.*

The Tale of Thomas Mead, Pat Hutchins. Mulberry Books, 1980.*

Tar Beach, Faith Ringgold. Crown Publishers, 1991.*

There's an Ant in Anthony, Bernard Most. Mulberry Books, 1992.*

Three Names, Patricia MacLachlan. HarperCollins, 1991.*

Tongue Twisters, Charles Keller. Simon and Schuster, 1989.*

The True Story of the 3 Little Pigs, Jon Scieszka. Scholastic Inc., 1991.*

Up, Up and Away: A Book About Adverbs, Ruth Heller. Grosset and Dunlop, 1991.*

The Very Hungry Caterpillar, Eric Carle. Philomel, 1970.*

When Will I Read, Miriam Cohen. Dell Publishing, 1983.*

William Shakespeare, Ibi Lepscky. Barron's Educational Series, Inc., 1988.*

Your Best Friend, Kate. Pat Brisson. Bradbury Press, 1989.*

SPATIAL INTELLIGENCE LITERATURE

A quick visit to the library or bookstore shows how publishing houses have focused on lavishly illustrated picture books in recent years. The illustrations in many of the books on this list take my breath away and delight my students so that they go back to them over and over again during their silent reading time.

For students who favor the spatial intelligence, these books may provide the first positive avenue into reading and studying language. These students already see life in pictures, and these books, which visually complement language so beautifully, inspire and motivate them. Books that nurture the spatial intelligence include the lavishly illustrated books and picture books, pop-up books, comic books, and coloring books.

A Child's Book of Art, Great Pictures, First Words, Judy Micklethwait. Dorling Kindersley, 1993.*

African American Art for Young People, Samella Lewis. Hand Craft, 1991.*

All I See, Cynthia Rylant. Orchard Books, 1988.*

Alphabatics, Suse MacDonald. Macmillan, 1986.*

Art Lesson, Tomie dePaola. Putnam's Sons, 1989.*

The Big Orange Splot, Daniel Manus Pinkwater. Scholastic, 1981.*

Bill Peet, an Autobiography, Bill Peet. Houghton Mifflin, 1989.

The Children's Illustrated Atlas, Janie Louise Hunt. Templar, 1996.

The Color Box, Dayle Ann Dodds. Little, Brown and Co., 1992.*

Color Dance, Ann Jonas. Greenwillow Books, 1989.*

Colors, Philip Yenawine. Delacorte Press, 1991.*

Deep in the Forest, Brinton Turkle. Dutton, 1976.*

Emma, Wendy Kesselman. Harper and Row, 1980.*

Frederick, Leo Lionni. Pantheon, 1966.*

Georgia O'Keefe, Robyn Montana Turner. Little, Brown and Co., 1991.*

Getting to Know the World's Greatest Artists, Georgia O'Keefe, Mike Venezia.
    Children's Press, 1993.*

The Great Migration, Jacob Lawrence. HarperCollins, 1993.*

Harriet and the Promised Land, Jacob Lawrence. Simon and Schuster Books for Young
    Readers, 1993.*

Hidden Pictures, Linda Bolton. Dial Books, 1993.*

How to Live Forever, Colin Thompson. Alfred Knopf, 1995.*

I Spy, Jean Marzolla. Scholastic Inc., 1992.*

Inspirations: Stories About Women Artists, Leslie Sills. Albert Whitman and Co., 1989.*

Jack and the Beanstalk, Alan Garner. Doubleday, 1992.*

James and the Giant Peach, Roald Dahl. Disney Press, 1996.*

Kente Colors, Debbi Chocolate and John Ward. Walker and Co., 1996.*

Li'l Sis and Uncle Willie, Gwen Everett. National Museum of American Art, Smithsonian Institute, 1991.*

Lines, Philip Yenawine. Delacorte Press, 1991.*

Linnea in Monet's Garden, Christina Bjach. Farrar, Straus and Giroux, 1987.*

Miss Spider's Wedding, David Kirk. Scholastic Inc., 1995.*

Opt: An Illusionary Tale, Arline and Joseph Baum. Puffin Books, 1989.*

Pablo Picasso, Ibi Lepscky. Barron's, 1984.*

Pigs From A–Z, Arthur Geisert, Houghton Mifflin, 1996.

Puzzle Maps USA, Nancy L. Clouse. Henry Holt and Co., 1990.

The Rainbow Fish, Marcus Pfister. North South Books, 1992.*

Round Trip, Ann Jonas. Mulberry Books, 1990.*

Shapes, Philip Yenawine. Delacorte Press, 1991.*

The Silver Pony, Lyn Ward, Houghton Mifflin, 1992.

Something Special, David McPhail. Little, Brown and Co., 1988.*

The Stupids Step Out, Harry Allard. Houghton Mifflin, 1977.*

Talking With Artists, Pat Cummings. Bradbury Press, 1992.

13th Clue, Ann Jonas. Greenwillow Books, 1992.*

Topsy and Turvys, Peter Newell. Dover Publications, 1964.*

Van Gogh, Ernest Raboff. Harper and Row, 1988.*

Visual Magic, David Thomson. Dial Books, 1991.*

Where's Waldo: The Wildly Wonderful Activity Book. Candlewick, 1995.

Where the Wild Things Are, Maurice Sendak. Harper, 1984.*

MUSICAL INTELLIGENCE LITERATURE

I enjoy reading poetry to my students to provide examples of writing with a rhythm. And many prose books have a rhythmic quality that makes them fit the musical intelligence category. This list saves my classroom from being "music-free."

Books that nudge the music intelligence include books of poetry, books with sing-along tapes, songbooks, and books about musicians and music.

POETRY

Hailstones and Halibut Bones, Mary O'Neill. Doubleday, 1973.

Honey, I Love, Eloise Greenfield. Cromwell, 1978.

If I Ran the Zoo, Dr. Seuss. Random House, 1980.*

If I Were in Charge of the World and Other Worries, Judith Viorst. Atheneum, 1984.

Mother Goose, A Treasury of Best Loved Rhymes, Watty Piper. Platt, 1972.

The Night Before Christmas, Clement Moore. Holiday House, 1980.

Nightmares: Poems to Trouble Your Sleep, Jack Prelutsky. Greenwillow, 1976.

Out in the Dark and Daylight, Aileen Fisher. Harper, 1980.

The Random House Book of Poetry for Children, Jack Prelutsky. Random House, 1983.

When the Dark Comes Dancing: A Bedtime Poetry Book, Nancy Larrick. Philomel, 1983.

Where the Sidewalk Ends, Shel Silverstein. Harper, 1974.

PROSE

All Night, All Day, Ashley Bryan. Atheneum, 1991.*

Animalia, Graeme Base. Scholastic Inc., 1986.*

A Young Person's Guide to Music, Neil Ardley. Dorling Kindersley, 1996.

Apt. 3, Ezra Jack Keats. Macmillan Child Group, 1986.*

Barn Dance, John Archambault and Bill Martin Jr. Henry Holt and Co., 1986.*

Beethoven Lives Upstairs, Barbara Nichol. Orchard Books, 1993.*

Brass, Dee Fillegard. Children's Press, 1988.*

Brown Bear, Brown Bear, What Do You See?, Bill Martin Jr. Henry Holt and Co., 1992.*

The Cat in the Hat Songbook, Dr. Seuss. Random House, 1967.

Celie and the Harvest Fiddler, Vanessa and Valerie Flournoy. Tambourine Books, 1995.*

Charlie Parker Played Be Bop, Christopher Raschka. Orchard Books, 1992.*

Chicka Chicka Boom Boom, Bill Martin Jr. and John Archambault. Scholastic Inc., 1989.*

City Sounds, Rebecca Emberly. Little, Brown and Co., 1989.*

Dancing Dream, Terri Cohlene. Rourke Corporation, 1990.*

Dancing Masks of Africa, Christine Price. Scribner, 1975.

Geraldine, The Music Mouse, Leo Lionni. Pantheon, 1979.*

The Green Book, compiled by Jeff Green. Professional Desk Reference, Inc. Songs classified by subject.

Homemade Band, Hap Palmer. Crown Publishing Group, 1990.

Hush Little Baby, Margot Zemach. Dutton, 1976.*

I Like the Music, Leah Komaiko. Harper and Row, 1987.*

I Live in Music, Ntozake Shange. Stewart, Tambori and Chang, Inc., 1978.*

The Incredible Journey, Sheila Burnford. Little, Brown and Co., 1960.

The Jester Has Lost His Jingle, David Saltzman. The Jester Company Inc., 1995.*

Jolly Mon, Jimmy and Susannah Buffett. Harcourt Brace Jovanovich, 1988.*

Kids in Motion, Julie Weisman. Alfred Publishing, 1993.

Kids Make Music, Avery and Mantell Hart. Williamson Publishing, 1993.

The Library of Children's Song Classics, Amy Appleby and Peter Pickon. Amsco Publications, 1993.

The Little Band, James Sage. M. K. McElderry Books, 1991.*

Little Rabbit Foo Foo, Michael Rosen. Simon and Schuster Books for Young Readers, 1990.*

Making Musical Things, Ann Wiseman. Charles Scribner's & Son, 1979.

Mama Don't Allow, Thacher Hurd. Harper and Row, 1985.*

Mary Wore a Red Dress and Henry Wore His Green Sneakers, Merle Peek. Clarion Books/Ticknor and Fields, 1985.*

Max Found Two Sticks, Brian Pinkney. Simon and Schuster, 1994.*

Meet the Orchestra, Ann Hayes. Harcourt Brace Jovanovich, 1991.*

Mozart Tonight, Julie Downing. Bradbury Press, 1991.*

Musical Max, Robert Kraus. Simon and Schuster, 1990.*

Music for Everyone, Vera B. Williams. Mulberry Books, 1988.*

Nicholas Cricket, Joyce Maxner. Harper and Row, 1989.

The Old Banjo, Dennis Haseley. Aladdin Books/Macmillan, 1990.*

The Pearl, John Steinbeck. Barron's Educational Series, 1985.

Percussion, Dee Fillegard. Children's Press, 1987.*

The Philharmonic Gets Dressed, Karla Kuslein. Harper and Row, 1982.

Piggyback Songs, Jean Warren. Tatline Press, 1983.

Polar Bear, Polar Bear, What Do You Hear?, Bill Martin Jr. and Eric Carle.
    Henry Holt and Company, 1991.*

Raggin': A Story About Scott Joplin, Barbara Mitchell. Carolrhoda Books, 1987.

Rondo in C, Paul Fleischman. Harper and Row, 1988.*

Scott Gustafson's Animal Orchestra, Scott Gustafson. Contemporary Books, 1988.*

Sing a Song of Chimimia: A Guatemalan Folktale, Jane Anne Vokmer. Carolrhoda
    Books Inc., 1995.*

The Song and Dance Man, Karen Ackerman. Dragonfly Books, 1992.*

Strings, Dee Fillegard. Children's Press, 1988.*

Sylvester the Mouse With the Musical Ear, Adelaide Holl. Golden Press, 1963.*

Today Is Monday: The All Year-Long Songbook, Roslyn Rubin and Judy Wathen.
    Scholastic Inc., 1980.

Ty's One Man Band, Mildred Walter. Four Winds Press, 1980. *

What Instrument Is This?, Rosemarie Husherr. Scholastic Inc., 1992.*

Wheels on the Bus: The All Year-Long Songbook, Roslyn Rubin and Judy Wathen.
    Scholastic Inc., 1980.

When Clay Sings, Baylor Byrd. Aladdin Books/Macmillan, 1972.*

Wood-Hoopoe Willie, Virginia Kroll. Cambridge, 1992.*

Woodwinds, Dee Fillegard. Children's Press, 1987.*

BODILY-KINESTHETIC INTELLIGENCE LITERATURE

One of my great loves in teaching is sharing athletics and movement with students. Many of my students are on athletic teams and enjoy dancing, so the following books excited and helped them realize that athletics, dancing, and movement can also be fun in language form. I always try to balance stories between the genders to be sure I provide girls with role models of athletic women.

Books for bodily-kinesthetic learners include touch-and-feel books, pull-and-press books, practical how-to books, cookbooks, and craft-oriented books.

Alvin Ailey, Andrea Davis Pinkney. Hyperion Books for Children, 1993.*

Angelina Ballerina, Katherine Holabird and Helen Craig. Clarkson Potter Publications, 1983.*

Babe Ruth: Home Run Hero, Keith Brandt. Troll Associates, 1986.

The Balancing Girl, Bernice Rabe. Dutton, 1981.*

Bear Shadow, Frank Asch. Prentice Hall, 1985.*

The Bicycle Man, Allen Jay. Houghton Mifflin, 1982.*

Crictor, Tomi Ungerer. Harper & Row, 1983.*

The Dog That Pitched a No-Hitter, Matt Christopher. Trumpet Club, 1988.

Football, Sue Boulais. Bancroft-Sage Publishers, 1992.

Going to My Ballet Class, Susan Kuklin. Bradbury Press, 1989.*

Jump, Frog, Jump, Kalan Kalon. Greenwillow Books, 1981.*

Kids Around the World Cookbook, Deri Robins. Kingfisher Publishers, 1994.

Kristi Yamaguchi, Shiobhan Donohue. Lerner Publications Co., 1994.

Little Basketball Big Leaguers, Bruce Nash and Allan Zullo. Little Simon, 1991.

The Macmillan Book of Baseball Stories, Terry Egan, Stem Friedmann, and Mike Levine. Simon and Schuster for Young Readers, 1992.

Max, Rachel Isadora. Macmillan, 1976.*

Mirette on the High Wire, Emily McAully. G. P. Putnam's Sons, 1992.*

Miss Nelson Has a Field Day, Harry Allard. Houghton Mifflin, 1985.*

My Dad the Magnificent, Kristi Parker. Dutton Children's Books, 1990.*

My Mama Had a Dancing Heart, Libba Moore Gray. Orchard Books, 1995.*

Oliver Button Is a Sissy, Tomie dePaola. Harcourt Brace Jovanovich, 1979.*

Pretend You're a Cat, Jean Marzollo. Dial Books for Young Readers, 1990.*

Sports Pages, Arnold Adoff. Harper & Row, 1990.

The Story of the Olympics, Dave Anderson. Beech Tree Paperbacks, 1990.

Take Me Out to the Ballgame, Jack Norworth and Alec Gillman. Four Winds Press, 1990.*

Teammates, Peter Glenbrock. Harcourt Brace Jovanovich, 1990.*

Those Summers, Alibi. HarperCollins, 1996.*

The Three Little Pigs, Paul Galdone. Clarion Books, 1970.*

The Very Young Dancer, Jill Krementz. Knopf, 1976.*

The Young Basketball Player, Chris Mullin. Dorling Kindersley, 1995.

The Young Dancer, Darcey Bussell. Dorling Kindersley, 1994.

Wheel Away, Dayle Ann Dodds. Harper & Row, 1989.*

Scholastic Professional Books • Developing Students' Multiple Intelligences

INTERPERSONAL INTELLIGENCE LITERATURE

I often use these books to preface a social skills lesson or theme. Throughout the year, I have my students discuss friendship and difficult family issues. Learning how to work with their friends, compromise, and care about others are some of the most important skills I can teach my students. I know that if they don't acquire these skills early, they're bound for lives of interpersonal struggles.

By reading books that include characters who face interpersonal challenges and figure out how to solve their problems, I provide students with discussion starters about real-life situations. I'll always remember reading *There's a Boy in the Girl's Bathroom* by Louise Sachar and having a boy who was a behavioral challenge walk up to me and say, "I guess I'm kind of like George. I just figure everyone thinks I'm bad so I might as well act that way." This young boy proceeded to tell the class the same thing later during a discussion, opening a door to talking about how we usually act consistent with the expectations of others. I won't tell you that this boy suddenly changed his ways, but I do think he no longer thought of himself as "bad," which is half the battle in working with students who have behavior problems.

One of my all-time favorite adult books is *Emotional Intelligence* by Daniel Goleman. Reading it has reinforced how important it is to help students learn to handle their emotions and relate to others in a positive way. Literature that helps encourage interpersonal skills includes plays, choral-reading scripts, Reader's Theater, books about people, and interactive books.

A House Is a House for Me, Mary Ann Hoberman. Scholastic, 1978.*

The Bears' House, Marilyn Sachs. Doubleday, 1971.

The Best Christmas Pageant Ever, Barbara Robinson, Avon, 1973.

The Big Book for Peace, Lloyd Alexander. Dutton Books, 1990.

Bridge to Terabithia, Katherine Patterson. Avon, 1979.

Charlie and the Great Glass Elevator, Roald Dahl. Alfred Knopf, 1972.

Dexter, Clyde Robert Bulla. Cromwell, 1973.

Do Like Kyla, Angela Johnson. Orchard Books, 1990.*

The Faithful Friend, Robert D. San Souci. Simon and Schuster for Young Readers, 1995.*

Family Secrets: Five Very Important Stories, Susan Shreve. Knopf, 1979.

First One Foot, Now the Other, Tomie dePaola. Putnam, 1980.*

Fishing With Dad, Michael Rosen. Artisan, 1996.*

The Foundling Fox, Irina Korschunow. Harper & Row, 1984. *

From the Mixed-Up Files of Mrs. Basil E. Frankweiler, E. L. Konigsburg. Atheneum, 1980.

The Giving Tree, Shel Silverstein. HarperCollins, 1964.*

Guess How Much I Love You, Sam McBratney. Candlewick Press, 1994.*

Hap Palmer Favorites, Hap Palmer. Alfred Publishing Co., 1981.

Hot and Cold Summer, Johanna Hurwitz. Morrow, 1984.

House for Hermit Crab, Eric Carl. Picture Book Studio, 1987.*

How It Feels to Live With a Physical Disability, Jill Krementz. Simon and Schuster, 1992.

Interactions, Debbie Pincus. Good Apple, 1988.

Jamaica's Find, Juanita Havill. Houghton Mifflin, 1986.*

The Kids' Guide to Social Action, Barbara Lewis. Free Spirit Pub., 1991.

The Land of Many Colors, Klamath County YMCA Family Preschool. Scholastic Inc., 1993.*

Learning the Skills of Peacemaking, Naomi Drew. Jalmas Press, 1987.

Let's Go to the Art Museum, Virginia Leuy. Harry N. Abrams, Inc., 1983.*

Love You Forever, Robert Munsch. Firefly Book Ltd., 1986.*

Mama, Do You Love Me?, Barbara Joosse. Chronicle Books, 1991.*

Matthew and Tilly, Rebecca Jones. Dutton Children's Books, 1991.*

People, Peter Spier. A Doubleday Book for Young Readers, 1980.*

Play With Me, Marie Hall Ets. Viking Penguin, 1976.*

The Runaway Bunny, Margaret Wise Brown. HarperCollins, 1942.*

There's a Boy in the Girl's Bathroom, Louise Sachar. Random House, 1988.

Think of Something Quiet, Clare Cherry. David S. Lake, 1981.*

Think on Your Feet, Linda Schwartz. The Learning Works, 1987.

School Isn't Fair, Patricia Baeh. Four Winds Press, 1989.*

Tribes, Jeanne Gibbs. Center Source Publications, 1987

Two Good Friends, Judy Delton. Crown, 1986.*

We Are Best Friends, Aliki. Greenwillow Books, 1982.*

The Wind in the Willows, Kenneth Grahame. David and Charles, 1992.

Words Can Hurt You, Barbara Thomson. Addison-Wesley, 1993.*

INTRAPERSONAL INTELLIGENCE LITERATURE

These books focus on characters who have strong intrapersonal intelligence or provide a social and personal theme that can serve as a catalyst for class discussions or journal writing. Sometimes as I read one of the books to students, I have them make short journal entries as I go along and at the end. Because I feel it is important to value students' privacy, I promise them that I will not read their journal entries.

Intrapersonal intelligence is a very abstract concept for many students. Anecdotal examples of individuals who are intrapersonally intelligent help my students grasp what it means in their daily lives. Our discussions focus on how characters are able to figure out how they feel about specific topics, how they analyze what they know, and how they make decisions that aren't always popular but are right.

Abby, Jeannette Caines. Harper Trophy, 1984.*

A Chair for My Mother, Vera Williams. Greenwillow, 1982.*

All By Myself, Mercer Mayer. Western Publishing, 1983.*

All Kinds of Families, Norma Simon. Albert Whitman, 1976.*

An Ellis Island Christmas, Maxinne Leighton. Viking, 1992.

Anne Frank: The Diary of a Young Girl, Anne Frank. Pocket Books, 1952.

Arthur's Chicken Pox, Marc Brown. Little, Brown and Co., 1994.*

Be a Perfect Person in Just Three Days, Stephen Manes. Bantam, 1984.

Big Al, Andrew Clements. Scholastic Inc., 1991.*

The Big Red Barn, Eve Bunting. Harcourt, 1979.*

Black Is Brown Is Tan, Arnold Adoff. Harper & Row, 1973.*

The Blanket That Had to Go, Nancy Cooney. G. P. Putnam's Sons, 1981.*

Broderick, Edward Ormondroyd. Houghton Mifflin, 1984.*

By Myself, David Kherdian. Henry Holt & Co., 1993.*

Call It Courage, Armstrong Sperry. Macmillan, 1971.

The Cay, Theodore Taylor. Doubleday, 1969.

Child of the Owl, Laurence Yep. Harper & Row, 1977.

The Courage of Sarah Noble, Alice Dalgliesh. Scribner, 1974.

Feelings, Alibi. Greenwillow Books, 1984.*

Feelings, Richard Allington and Kathleen Cowles. Raintree, 1991.*

Grandfather's Journey, Allen Say. Houghton Mifflin, 1993.*

The Grouchy Lady Bug, Eric Carle. Scholastic, Inc., 1977.*

Happy Birthday, Martin Luther King, Jean Marzolla. Scholastic Inc., 1993.*

Harry and the Terrible Watzit, Dick Gackenbach. Clarion, 1984.*

Helping Out, George Ancona. Clarion Books, 1985.*

Here I Am an Only Child, Marlene Shyer. Aladdin, 1985.*

How the Other Half Lives, Jacob Riis. Dover Publications, Inc., 1971.

I Am Not a Crybaby, Norma Simon. Puffin Books, 1989.*

I Like Me, Nancy Carlson. Viking, 1988.*

I Love My Family, Nade Hudson. Scholastic Inc., 1993.*

I'm Terrific, Marjorie Sharmat. Holiday House, 1977.*

I Never Saw Another Butterfly, Hana Volvavkova. Schocken Books, 1993.

Inside My Feet: The Story of a Giant, Richard Kennedy. Harper, 1979.

Island of the Blue Dolphins, Scott O'Dell. Houghton Mifflin, 1960.

The It-Doesn't-Matter Suit, Sylvia Plath. St. Martin's Press, 1996.

I Was So Mad!, Norma Simon, Albert Whitman & Co., 1974.*

Julie of the Wolves, Jean Craighead George. Harper & Row, 1972.

Lafcadio, The Lion Who Shot Back, Shel Silverstein. Harper, 1963.

Lassie Come Home, Rosemary Wells and Susan Jeffers. Henry Holt and Co., 1995.*

Leo the Late Bloomer, Robert Kraus. Simon and Schuster, 1971.*

Memories of My Life in a Polish Village, Toby Knoble Fluek. Alfred A. Knopf, 1990.

Missing May, Cynthia Rylant. Orchard Books, 1992.

The Mixed-Up Chameleon, Eric Carle. HarperCollins, 1984.*

Molly's Pilgrim, Barbara Cohen. Lothrop, 1983.

Mr. and Mrs. Smith Have Only One Child, But What a Child, Cecile Bertrand. Lothrop, Lee and Shepard, 1992.*

My Mother's House, My Father's House, C. B. Christiansen. Atheneum, 1989.*

My Twin Sister Erika, Ilse-Margaret Vogel. Harper, 1976.

Nana Upstairs, Nana Downstairs, Tomie dePaola. G. P. Putnam's Sons, 1973.*

The Number on My Grandfather's Arm, David A. Adler. UAHC Press, 1987.

Peace Begins With You, Katherine Scholes. Little Brown and Co., 1990.*

Pig William, Arlene Dubanevich. Bradbury Press, 1985.*

Quick as a Cricket, Audrey Wood. Child's Play, 1982.*

Roll of Thunder; Hear My Cry, Mildred Taylor. Dial Press, 1976.

Say Hello, Vanessa, Marjorie Sharmat. Holiday House, 1979.*

Shy Charles, Rosemary Wells. Dial, 1988.*

The Shy Little Girl, Phyllis Krasilovsky. Scholastic Inc., 1992.*

The Sign of the Beaver, Elizabeth George Speare. Dell Publishing, 1983.

Sometimes I Like to Be Alone, Heidi Geonnel. Little, Brown, & Co., 1989.*

The Story of Ferdinand, Munro Leaf. Scholastic Inc., 1964.*

The Tenth Good Thing About Barney, Judith Viorst. Atheneum, 1975.*

The Very Quiet Cricket, Eric Carle. Philomel Books, 1990.*

We Are All Alike, We Are All Different, Cheltenham Elementary School Kindergartners. Scholastic, Inc., 1991.*

We Can Do It!, Laura Dwight. Checkerboard Press, 1992.*

When I Was Little, Jamie Lee Curtis. HarperCollins, 1993.*

When the New Baby Comes I'm Moving Out, Martha Alexander. Dial, 1981.*

Where the Red Fern Grows, Wilson Rawls. Bantam, 1974.

Year of Impossible Goodbyes, Sook Nyul Choi. Houghton Mifflin, 1991.

You Are Much Too Small, Betty Boegehold. Bantam Books, 1990.*

Developing Students' Multiple Intelligences • Scholastic Professional Books

Chapter 6

The Multiple Intelligences Classroom: A Place for Active Learning

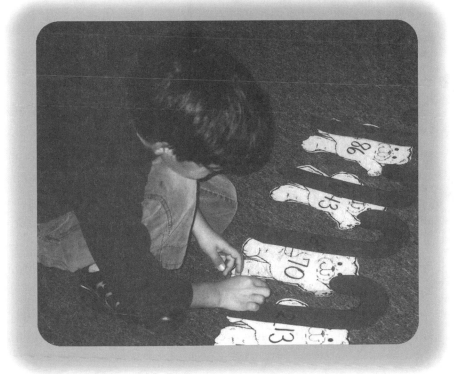

A classroom that integrates multiple intelligences into the daily hustle and bustle of learning and management is a unique and special place. The teacher no longer simply imparts knowledge and rules to students, and students are no longer empty vessels waiting to be filled. Instead, the teacher is a facilitator or coach who oversees the students' learning process. Students are active learners who play a critical role in their own learning as they create projects, work with others, and use their own learning styles to succeed. As I began to experience these changes in roles, I realized that the physical space of my classroom had to be changed. I knew it was not enough to provide my students with a desk and chair facing the front of the classroom. They needed working space that offered them access to the various tools required to engage in serious learning using many different modalities. I needed to think of my classroom as a collection of work stations and personal-learning areas rather than a simple space dedicated to disseminating information.

It's important to recognize the influence that the physical environment has on student learning. Students who walk into a classroom that is print-rich, and full of bright colors and student work—and that includes individual work spaces, small-group areas, and an area for whole-class instruction—will see their learning environment as a positive place. Students' involvement in their learning increases when they can move about and experience learning for themselves. Consider the "affective domain" of physical environment. Think of rooms, offices, classrooms, and homes that you consider wonderful places to be. Now think of the local dentist office—sterile, quiet except for the drill, bland colors, and poor lighting.

ESTABLISHING A SUPPORTIVE CLASSROOM ATMOSPHERE

Before concentrating on the physical space, it's important to look at the social world that provides the foundation of the classroom atmosphere. In the classroom that uses multiple intelligences strategies, students need to feel that talk and collaboration are acceptable behavior. They need to feel that working alone in a private space is always an option.

To create a classroom atmosphere where students feel safe, important, and free to explore and enjoy learning, you need to establish a set of rules of participation that guide your students' behavior whether in teacher-led, whole-class lessons; small-group sessions; or independent work time. If the rules reflect that both social and individual efforts contribute to learning, they're likely to be relevant to a wide range of student backgrounds. And it's important that students be involved in deciding on these rules so that they'll have a stake in following them. Some of the rules my students and I have chosen include:

- **Listen when the teacher or classmates are talking to you.**
- **Give your classmates a chance to talk.**
- **Ask your classmates for their ideas.**
- **Contribute your own ideas.**
- **Try to figure things out for yourself. When you can't, ask your classmates first and then your teacher.**
- **Treat everyone with respect.**

Once you and your students have established a set of rules, you'll need to model them consistently, using both positive and negative examples.

THE PHYSICAL ARRANGEMENT

Whatever the size or physical setting of your classroom, arranging the room to reinforce the multiple intelligences is a difficult and challenging task. The social environment of the classroom has to be reinforced by a physical arrangement that is flexible enough to change quickly, allowing students to learn in the following three ways:

- **in a whole-class setting;**
- **in small groups where they can talk and work together for part of the day;**
- **in individual nooks and learning centers where they can work alone.**

Keeping in mind that the physical arrangement of a classroom is always temporary, think about how to arrange your classroom furniture to accommodate the three learning approaches. Most classrooms I've visited have the large- and small-group arrangements. The challenge is to also include smaller, private areas for students to work in alone or with one other person. If space allows, it's also beneficial to have an area for students to create dances, work on skits, and learn in other bodily-kinesthetic ways. It's also necessary to take into consideration that students will need to move around the

This cute bulletin board represents an interpersonal and multicultural theme as students "look out" upon the world of people working together.

classroom without disrupting the general flow of instruction and learning.

As you begin to visualize the myriad of classroom arrangements, be sure to give your students a voice in the process. Many students, especially those gifted in spatial intelligence, will be thrilled to sketch a blueprint for rearranging the classroom. Take the time to explain to students the important issues to consider, and you may be surprised to find that certain students will come up with all sorts of creative ideas you hadn't considered for rearranging the room. And they'll do it on a regular basis. For example, after years of teaching, it was difficult for me to see a bookcase as anything but a bookcase. Yet students taught me that a bookcase could also close off spaces, house science projects, and stand in the middle of the classroom as a "free-floating rectangle" during geometry month.

A comfortable, private reading center is created by closing off space with a bookshelf and storage cabinets and adding a couple of bean-bag chairs.

ARRANGING THE CLASSROOM ARTFULLY

Thinking of artists' work brings to mind beautiful paintings, music, and writing that opens up new worlds. A classroom can be seen as a blank page waiting for an artist's touch. Some classrooms I've seen take my breath away while others generate the wish to escape after a brief visit. Here are a few ideas that can help make a classroom a piece of art.

ARRANGING THE FURNITURE

Just as artists start with a selection of colors and a blank piece of paper, you start with what you are given—a particular space and furniture commonly found in classrooms throughout the nation. You are likely to have student desks, a few tables and bookshelves, a teacher's desk, chairs, computer booths, and—in the lower grades—rugs and pillows. But the artist's eye sees what each piece brings to a classroom as well as the potential for adding a few items

A simple listening center, placed behind a storage cabinet, features a round table that has been lowered so that students can sit on the floor as they listen to a story.

that can make a big difference.

In arranging furniture, ask yourself: Will this arrangement lend itself to whole-class instruction? Small-group work? Individual work? Are there well-defined spaces where students can work without being disturbed? How can I use a bookcase, a table, or a computer nook to help define space?

Think about what new pieces of furniture could enhance the space. Consider: milk crates, bookshelves on wheels, low tables, throw rugs, an old coffee table, a rocking chair, bean bag chairs, beach chairs, revolving bookcases, book racks, message boards, small couches, portable chalkboards, and seat cushions. I've seen a teacher use an ironing board for a corner puppet theater, a tent for a reading corner, and round tables and cubbies for student desks. One of my favorite classrooms has benches arranged near the blackboard for whole-group discussions and a series of

work stations arranged throughout the room. These stations are separated from one another by tall bookcases and file cabinets. And students have baskets for their belongings and designated spots in the room where they keep their baskets and backpacks.

Start your planning by facing the fact that some furniture is either immovable or would be very difficult to move. You'll need to recognize these pieces at the beginning of the year so that you can place them in spots that can complement most classroom arrangements. Examples include a teacher's desk, storage shelves, and built-in cabi-

A meeting area is created so students can "meet privately" for discussions and activities in a comfortable environment.

nets and shelving. You'll also need to take into consideration the characteristics of the room that you can't change, such as the locations of the coat closet, supply closet, and windows. These may be fixtures, but even these can be transformed in creative ways. I know a teacher who took the door to the coat closet off and used the closet as a private reading nook. With added lighting, these spaces can become private reading areas or—with a small table—a writing center. A colleague of mine designed a popular writing

A private reading center is closed off from the rest of the classroom, providing a comfortable place for students to lay on a large pillow and read.

center that included a desk with a large piece of cardboard cut out in the shape of a pencil attached to its side so that students had to "climb into the pencil" to get in.

Children of all ages love private areas. Who can't remember building forts or designing special play corners to have our own space. If your classroom doesn't have the space for these nooks, a few simple props can turn a student desk into a private area. For example, you can cut refrigerator boxes into large, movable rectangles and place them between facing student desks to provide two private areas. Or consider laminating manila folders to use as dividers between students.

A private writing center is created by placing a revolving bookshelf and a large bookcase around a table.

PROVIDING PRIVATE SPACES

Providing students with those private and individual spaces is essential to a classroom that uses multiple intelligences strategies.

A verbal-linguistic center is created with comfortable children's seats and stuffed animals. Tape recorders and headsets are stored in crates on the floor.

These special spaces nurture the affective domain, empowering students and enhancing learning. Still, finding enough private spaces for students has been a constant challenge for me because I usually have 30 students in my class. Yet as I began to let students know that giving them their own space—no matter how small—is a priority for me, it became a priority for students to respect and take care of these spaces. For example, one year when I had 35 students I allowed a student to work at my own desk several times each week. The student was proud to be working there and took care to clean up and keep things in order.

One of the most common frustrations I've heard from students is the feeling of being crowded. Many arguments and conflicts between students arise because of the sense of powerlessness that comes with not having a personal space or feeling that their space can be violated. The feeling of being crowded is often caused by student desks being placed too close together so that pathways around the desks are too tight. Consequently, students run into one another or knock things off desks. To decrease this frustration, take special care to arrange student desks so they are not tightly packed. If you're teaching in a small classroom or have many students, you may need to get rid of any pieces of furniture you don't absolutely need. Even when you arrange desks apart to provide students with space, desks can shift by the end of a busy day of learning. Train yourself to notice this so that you and your students can put

A Literature Center is designed with reference books and plenty of table space for student work. Donated benches are used instead of chairs.

things back in place during the day.

Another cause of the crowding frustration is the use of table desks: two students share one table with two separate cubby holes attached. This is tremendously upsetting to a neat student who is forced to sit next to the classroom slob and spends most of the day pushing the slob's books and papers out of his way. If your classroom has shared desks, have students put a piece of tape down the middle to define personal space, and talk frequently to students about neatness and organization.

CONTROLLING CLASSROOM TRAFFIC

Space to move around in is essential for any classroom. But it's especially critical for MI classrooms, which include lessons that depend on different approaches to working with information. Students have to be able to easily move to and from learning and materials-storage centers throughout the day as well as get in and out of the classroom and in general move around without bumping into one another. To avoid classroom congestion, it's important to establish clearly defined pathways to help movement become a natural part of the classroom instead of a disruption.

Students have to clearly understand which areas of the classroom are learning and working areas and which are pathways for movement. If they don't, all sorts of chaos can occur. For example, if a student decides to plop down in the pathway to work on an independent activity, it is only a matter of time until another student will disrupt the activity as he maneuvers around the student.

DISTRIBUTING MATERIALS

You can store materials in a central place in the classroom or place them in numerous spots around the room. These materials may include:

- **Basics — paper, construction paper, pens, pencils, scissors, tape, rulers, etc.**
- **Tools — measuring devices, calculators, microscopes, etc.**
- **Containers — envelopes, boxes, racks, pails, etc.**
- **Information Sources — references, pictures, recordings, natural specimens, labels, books, charts, magazines, etc.**

I've found that having all materials in a centralized place can lead to what I call the "wandering soul syndrome"— students use their frequent journeys to the supply center to chat with classmates and procrastinate. One way to reduce the wandering soul syndrome is to decentralize materials that are used on a regular basis. This might mean placing paper, pens, scissors, and other frequently used materials in several locations around the room. Those materials that aren't used as much can be centralized to save space.

AVOIDING OVERSTIMULATION

It's important to create a colorful, stimulating classroom. But some classrooms are "overdone" with too much student work and too many posters and sayings adorning the walls. It's easy to identify those classrooms because when I visit them, I quickly feel overstimulated. As the teacher chats with me, I find my eyes roaming the four walls to study student work, examine posters, and ponder quotes. It takes most of my mental energy to simply stand there and take it all in, and at the end of the visit, I have little or no idea of what the teacher has told me.

How can students possibly concentrate on learning when their senses are being constantly bombarded by so many colors, pictures, and words? The lesson to remember is it's not how much is on the walls but what is on the walls that counts. Leaving some blank spaces on the walls and on the floor offers students a break from the stimulation and can give a classroom a breath of fresh air.

BRIDGING THE PHYSICAL AND SOCIAL ENVIRONMENTS

The social environment of the classroom will always determine the physical environment. At certain times in the year, you'll need to focus on whole-group instruction and at other times on centers and small groups. During the working-together times, students are likely to become too social, and you'll need to pull in the reigns and rearrange the classroom to offer more private spaces and fewer group areas. If students aren't following the classroom rules, discuss the issues in a class

In the Ancient History Research Center, students use the laser discs, computers, maps, and one another to access and analyze information.

meeting and explain that you'll have to rearrange the room until they are able to follow these important rules.

The curriculum also plays a role in classroom arrangements. During the months I focus on writing workshops, which require a lot of peer meetings and peer editing, I arrange my room to include more open small-group areas and fewer specific-activity centers. Conversely, during science units that require independent lab work, centers become more important.

An Art Center is formed by closing off space using a bookshelf, a trash can, and a long table.

ENSURING A MULTIPLE INTELLIGENCES ENVIRONMENT

Many classroom environments center naturally on verbal-linguistic and mathematical-logical intelligences. Bulletin boards, posters, and room arrangements are based upon these intelligences, especially the verbal-linguistic. To make sure that all intelligences are represented in your classroom environment, use the following checklist:

INTERPERSONAL INTELLIGENCE

- **Do students have opportunities and physical areas to interact with one another?**
- **Can students find areas to have a conversation without disturbing others?**
- **Is there ample space for group work?**
- **Are there procedures for conflict mediation to help students learn to work together?**
- **Do feelings of respect and trust pervade the classroom?**

Developing Students' Multiple Intelligences • Scholastic Professional Books

INTRAPERSONAL INTELLIGENCE

- **Do students have areas in the classroom where they know they can go to work alone and undisturbed?**
- **Is there respect for privacy?**
- **Do students feel accepted enough to take time and space for reflection?**
- **Do students feel it's okay to share their feelings and opinions?**
- **Do students have opportunities to choose activities?**

SPATIAL INTELLIGENCE

- **Is the classroom arranged to accommodate different learning styles?**
- **Are there desks, tables, floor areas, and private study areas?**
- **Do colors in the room stimulate students' senses?**
- **Is the room well lit or are there dark areas?**
- **Is there ample open space so that students don't feel crowded?**
- **Are there a variety of visual experiences?**

BODILY-KINESTHETIC INTELLIGENCE

- **Can students move around in the classroom and not be at their desks the entire day?**
- **Are there materials that allow students to build, design, and have hands-on experiences?**
- **Are there spaces for students to perform and practice plays?**

A Chess Center provides a quiet place to learn and play. This center is closed off by a bookcase and a storage cabinet.

MUSICAL INTELLIGENCE

- Is the auditory environment conducive to learning?
- Is there background music for students at times?
- Do I fluctuate my teaching voice?
- Do I express or acknowledge an interest in music and rhythm in my teaching?
- Is there an area of the room where students can use headphones to explore music and sounds?

VERBAL-LINGUISTIC INTELLIGENCE

- Do words on the classroom walls challenge students' growing vocabulary?
- Is there so much exposure to words that students are overstimulated?
- Does too much talking—by me and/or the students—go on in the classroom?

MATHEMATICAL-LOGICAL INTELLIGENCE

- Is there logical and consistent sequencing of activity each day?
- Are there if-then consequences that are easy to follow?
- Are transition times organized and orderly?
- Are there opportunities for students to explore mathematical instruments (calculators, protractors, manipulatives)?
- Are science materials available for students to work with outside of science lessons?

A bodily-kinesthetic math center is placed in the corner of a room where students are able to shoot a basket each time they answer a math problem correctly.

Developing Students' Multiple Intelligences • Scholastic Professional Books

Sample Classroom Layout #1

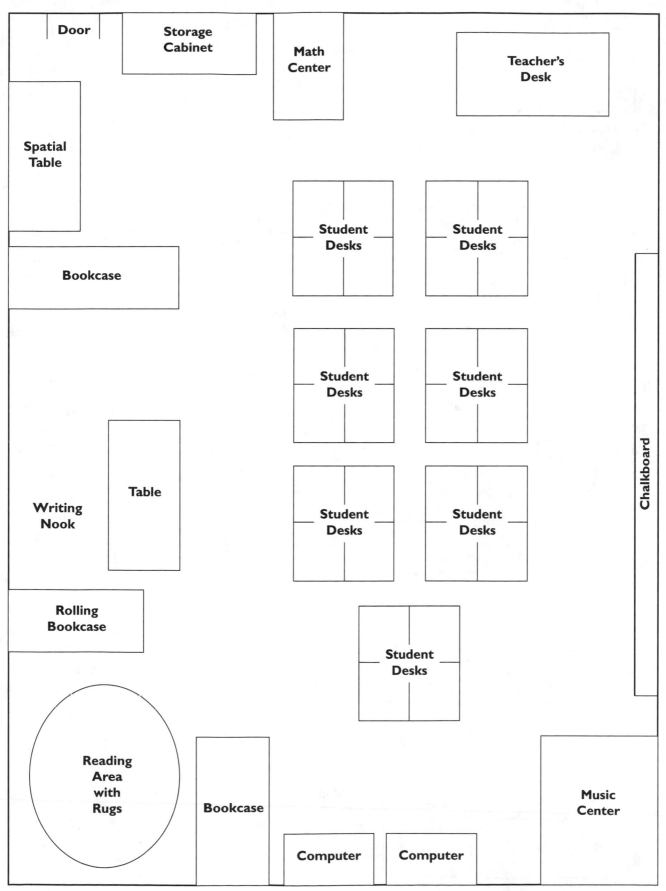

Scholastic Professional Books • Developing Students' Multiple Intelligences

Sample Classroom Layout #2

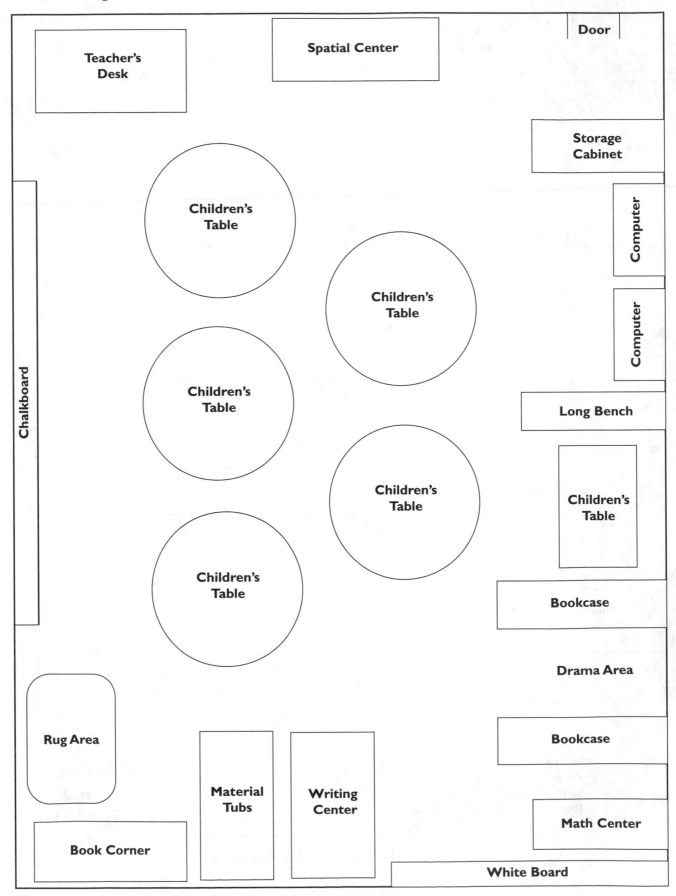

Teacher's Desk

Spatial Center

Door

Storage Cabinet

Computer

Computer

Chalkboard

Children's Table

Children's Table

Children's Table

Children's Table

Children's Table

Long Bench

Children's Table

Bookcase

Drama Area

Bookcase

Rug Area

Material Tubs

Writing Center

Math Center

Book Corner

White Board

Chapter 7

Multiple Intelligences Assessment Strategies

Teaching with multiple intelligences has forced me to reexamine my assessment strategies and bring them more in line with the type of teaching and learning going on in my classroom. I've worked to change in two areas of assessment:

• Assessing students' academic and social growth
• Assessing students' strengths and weaknesses in the multiple intelligences areas

Assessing students through the lense of multiple intelligences challenges us to see students as unique individuals. I've found that using multiple assessment measures that include both performance-based and norm-based evaluation tools gives me a more accurate picture of each student. My goal is to identify what students know and can do and identify gaps and weaknesses so that I can tailor instruction to draw on all areas and strengthen the weaker ones.

ASSESSING STUDENTS' MULTIPLE INTELLIGENCES GROWTH

The foundation of my assessment of students' growth in the multiple intelligences is to observe them at work. If students are strengthening their intelligences through the opportunities I give them within the curriculum, then their grades and academic achievement levels should demonstrate the progress they're making. If their grades and work levels are not improving, I take it as a reflection of the type of activities I'm providing. After all, if students are able to learn using their natural mental and social abilities, then their understanding of concepts and retention of knowledge should benefit directly.

For example, a few years ago one of my students started the year "hating" math and his grades showed it. He lacked the skills and knowledge to experience success. I began to provide math activities that drew on his strengths in spatial and verbal-linguistic intelligences. As he began to visualize the math concepts through his drawings and to write about math concepts, his understanding of math increased. By March he had a solid B in math and, although he still claimed that he "hated" it, he'd stopped his groaning and complaining months earlier. When it came time for assessment, his math work showed great improvement in three intelligences: math-logic, spatial, and verbal-linguistic.

In addition to observation, I use a broad array of techniques to assess students' academic growth with an eye to their multiple intelligences development. These include standardized tests, classroom tests and assignments, portfolio work showing student work in all intelligence and curriculum areas, student self-reflections and goal-setting sheets, anecdotal records, and parental assessment of their child's development. The information I obtain through this variety of techniques helps me get the most accurate picture possible of the strengths and weaknesses of each student.

The next step is to use my knowledge about the students' MI strengths to tailor lessons that will help them use other intelligences to learn and understand more in the curriculum areas. An important weekly goal for me is to see students improve in a specific academic area by using and applying their multiple intelligences. Not only am I assessing students' academic growth, but I am gaining valuable information about how they are using their different intelligences in productive activities.

THINGS TO KEEP IN MIND WHEN ASSESSING MULTIPLE INTELLIGENCES

Here are some of the conclusions I've drawn as I've learned more about multiple intelligences and how the brain works. I think about these as I plan instruction and assessment.

- **Intelligence is not fixed or static at birth.**

- **Intelligence can be learned, taught, and enhanced.**

- **Intelligence is a multidimensional phenomenon that is present at multiple levels of our brain/mind/body system.**

- **Individual student and teacher differences need to be accepted and nurtured.**

- **Children grow and develop as a whole, neither one skill or talent at a time nor at the same rate for each skill and talent.**

- **Each student is a multiply intelligent and talented individual in both academic and nonacademic areas.**

- **Students need to learn to problem-solve, find and work with information, absorb content, and think critically about issues and solutions.**

Several multiple intelligences experts have developed continuums to assess how the intelligences grow as they are used in productive activities. These include: David Lazear's "Basic to Complex Coherence Level" described in his 1994 book *Multiple Intelligences Approaches to Assessment* and Bruce Campbell's "Novice-Apprentice-Practitioner-Scholar" continuum presented in his 1994 book *The Multiple Intelligences Handbook.* I've chosen to assess students' growth and intelligences improvement through the work they're doing in my classroom. I recommend that you start off slowly and begin simply by observing student work and improvement. Gradually, you'll become aware of other assessment tools and broaden your techniques.

Several schools have developed report cards that integrate the academic areas with the multiple intelligences. Since my school hasn't, I use the comment section on each student's report card to discuss his or her growth in the multiple intelligences. I send home a separate profile sheet within the formal report card, which I usually fill out at a private conference with each student. I've found that these conferences are a powerful way to help students learn to assess themselves and their work. (See the Multiple Intelligences Report Profile at the end of this chapter.)

MULTIPLE INTELLIGENCES PORTFOLIOS

One of the easiest starting points for increasing the array of assessments you use in your classroom is to use portfolios. Portfolios are valuable assessment tools because they consist of a well-planned collection of student work done throughout the year. They provide a clear and comprehensive view of the caliber of work students are producing, the intelligences and curricular subjects in which they are improving, and the areas that need attention. When you review them, student growth and academic improvement is either very evident or it isn't. There is no hiding behind a "bad" testing day or an assignment that received too much parental help. At times I've been in the middle of filling out a student's report card and come to a borderline grade that could go either way. By pulling out the student's portfolio, I can easily make a decision and formulate an articulate comment.

As well as being an effective assessment tool for you, portfolios provide important information for parents and for students:

For parents. Portfolios help to make parent conferences objective rather than subjective. No longer will a parent leave a conference thinking you "don't like" their child or that you're "going easy" on her. Portfolios provide a body of work that speaks for itself—good, bad, or indifferent.

For students. Portfolios are valuable self-assessment tools for students. It's important to let students see their portfolios at any time and allow them to add work to them at any time. Being in charge of their portfolios, students will soon acquire a sense of ownership of their academic and social growth and improvements.

TYPES OF PORTFOLIOS

There's no one way to use portfolios in your classroom. The ideas in the following list are just suggestions. You may choose to have several types of portfolios going on throughout the year or may want to focus on just one or two. Throughout the year, I use showcase and archive portfolios, which I keep in two large boxes near my desk. At the same time, I have students keep their own multiple intelligences portfolios, which they turn in at the end of each quarter. Occasionally I use the single subject portfolio for students who want to monitor their progress in a specific subject or area. As we've gained technology resources in our school, I've begun to use video portfolios to provide a visual record of student growth.

Showcase Portfolios. These include selected pieces of students' best work. Students know that the showcase portfolio gives them a way to show off what they can do and what they've learned. Knowing their parents will be seeing this portfolio throughout the year, most students are eager to develop them well.

Archive Portfolios. These include a wide variety of student work—rough drafts, planning sheets, self-reflection activities, and completed student work. The purpose of the archive portfolio is to show student growth and improvement over time. Therefore, not everything in this type of portfolio looks great or has wonderful grades. For me, the archive portfolio is the most valuable tool for assessment.

Multiple Intelligences Portfolios. Multiple intelligences portfolios include student work in all the intelligence areas. I require students to have a work example of each intelligence in the portfolio at all times. If the work they wish to include is a three-dimensional project, they put a written explanation in the portfolio. All items need to be clearly marked with the applicable intelligence(s). I give students freedom to replace, add, or compile examples of their multiple intelligences work.

Single Subject Portfolios. Single subject portfolios are dedicated to a specific curriculum area—language, math, science, or social studies.

Developing Students' Multiple Intelligences • Scholastic Professional Books

Videotape Portfolios. At the beginning of the year, each student donates a video-tape, clearly labeled with his or her name. Taped entries fall into two categories: formal and informal. I usually have five formal entries on each student's videotape. These show the student solving a problem or giving a presentation. I stay with these two types to provide a consistent record of growth and improvement. Also included on the tape are the student's responses to my higher-level questions, designed to make them evaluate or analyze the problem they've just solved or the presentation they've just made. After every second formal entry, I send the videotape home for parents to watch.

Informal taped entries can be more varied in content. For example, sometimes when students are working with a partner or in a group, I'll grab their videotape and tape the activity. These informal entries provide solid evidence of how the student is growing socially. The videotape is an-end-of-the year gift for each student. Parents and students love the videotape portfolios, and I have no problem recruiting parents to help organize the tapes as well as help with the actual taping.

Electronic Portfolios. Technology-literate teachers who have access to computers and a scanner can use these tools to create highly effective electronic portfolios. Kept on the computer, these show student work just like a regular portfolio. Students can type work directly into the computer or use a scanner. They can also create desktop publishing presentations.

ASSESSING STUDENTS' MULTIPLE INTELLIGENCES STRENGTHS AND WEAKNESSES

In the past few years, several assessments to determine which intelligences students are strong in and which ones offer the greatest challenges have been developed. These include the Teele Inventory of Multiple Intelligences (TIMI), the Rogers Inventory of Multiple Intelligences (RIMI), Project Spectrum, and the numerous assessment tools developed by David Lazear.

Knowing students' natural strengths and weaknesses in the multiple intelligences is important because it helps teachers design lessons and work with students on a meaningful and challenging level. But I do have some concerns about the use of these assessments. Rather than simply accept the assessment methods set down for us, it's important that we be clear about what we are trying to accomplish with assessment.

ASSESSMENT MEASURES OF STUDENTS' MULTIPLE INTELLIGENCES

I base my measures of students' intelligences on several sources of information. Although this may seem to add time and effort, it helps me examine why I'm doing activities in my classroom and how I can use them for assessment. Here are five of the assessment measures I use:

Pie Chart Activity. I have students rank their intelligences by labeling each slice of a pie chart with an intelligence. In each area, they draw a few pictures of how they use that intelligence and then rank each area with a number from one to ten. One represents an intelligence that they'd like to be stronger in, and ten represents an area they are confident about.

Student Questionnaire. Students complete a Student MI Questionnaire (see sample at the end of this chapter) on which they give examples and details regarding their own assessment of their intelligences. I give the questionnaire to students at the beginning of the year and again at the end of the year.

Parent Questionnaire. Parents answer questions about their view of their child's intelligences, providing a historical perspective. (See the sample at the end of this chapter.)

Classroom Information. Observations, classroom tests, and parent-student-teacher conferences are other ways to assess students' strengths and weaknesses. Observation alone is a powerful way to assess students. Gardner suggests that classrooms provide a myriad of multiple intelligences activities and materials and that teachers watch kids in this environment to see what the child is attracted to and what he or she can do.

Teacher Assessment. After I've worked with students for a couple of months, I assess each student based on all of the information I have gathered. Finally I compare my assessment, the student's self-assessment, and the parent assessment to find the major similarities. I usually find that all three assessments are similar and provide me with a good overall picture of the student's strengths and weaknesses.

However you choose to assess students' intelligences, the main purpose is for you, parents, and the students to gain a deeper understanding of the student's natural proclivities and intelligences. Once you have this information, you can begin tailoring lessons to help students achieve using their strong intelligences while strengthening their weaker ones.

Developing Students' Multiple Intelligences • Scholastic Professional Books

Multiple Intelligences Report Profile for_____

(1 = low interest and skill; 2 = beginning interest and some skill; 3 = showing growth in skills and creations; 4 = consistent growth in skill level and interest; 5 = high interest and excellent skills)

Verbal-Linguistic   1   2   3   4   5
Comments:

Math-Logic   1   2   3   4   5
Comments:

Spatial   1   2   3   4   5
Comments:

Bodily-Kinesthetic   1   2   3   4   5
Comments:

Musical   1   2   3   4   5
Comments:

Interpersonal   1   2   3   4   5
Comments:

Intrapersonal   1   2   3   4   5
Comments:

Overall comments regarding student's growth in the multiple intelligences areas:

Multiple Intelligences Assessment Concerns

Just one tool is inadequate for assessing students' intelligences.

While all of these multiple intelligences assessment instruments are valid tools, I believe that giving students one of them and making overall generalizations about their intelligences can be short-sighted and statistically unsound. In the case of self-ranking assessments, I can think of dozens of students who've assessed themselves high in areas that interest them yet ranked themselves low in their actual strengths. I've seen that some students tend to rank themselves high in bodily-kinesthetic, spatial, and interpersonal intelligences most of the time. And recent research has shown that elementary students do tend to be naturally strong in bodily-kinesthetic and spatial intelligences. Yet I have a hunch that students choose to rank themselves high in these areas because they enjoy sports and games more than reading, writing, and arithmetic. I do believe that it's important for students to assess their strengths and weaknesses. Yet I caution against using these self-assessments as an end in itself. It is important to use a balanced approach to assessing students' intelligences—an approach that includes achievement, classroom work, and natural proclivities.

It isn't necessary to assess primary students' multiple intelligences.

I choose to withhold any multiple intelligences assessment for K–2 students, whose self-concept and sense of themselves is just developing during these early years. I find that these younger students fluctuate most from month to month in assessing their intelligences. They tend to rank themselves high in an area that they've just completed and enjoyed. Older students seem much more consistent and accurate in their self-assessments. Many of my colleagues who teach primary grades prefer to assess students through observing them and assessing their classroom work and social behavior for a couple of weeks.

There's a danger of using multiple intelligences to label students.

In visiting MI classrooms, I've heard students make such comments as, "I'm a spatially intelligent student." And I've heard teachers make similar comments, "John isn't very verbally-linguistic intelligent but he is truly a bodily-kinesthetic intelligent student." This type of conversation implies that the multiple intelligences are being taught as separate entities, not the interdependent parts of the brain that they truly are.

All students have multiple intelligences. All students have all of the intelligences. Our assessment measures should show and report how each intelligence is used in productive activities—not become just another way of labeling students and putting them in separate boxes.

Developing Students' Multiple Intelligences • Scholastic Professional Books

Student MI Questionnaire

Please complete the following questions as honestly as you can. There are no right or wrong answers!

1. What is your favorite subject in school? _____

2. What are your hobbies and interests outside of school?

_____

3. Check all of the things you think you are good at:

_____ **Reading**
_____ **Writing**
_____ **Speaking in front of others or in small groups**
_____ **Art (drawing, painting, sculpting, etc.)**
_____ **Music (singing, listening to music, playing an instrument, etc.)**
_____ **Math (calculating, measuring, solving logic problems, etc.)**
_____ **Movement Activities (dancing, acting, playing sports, etc.)**
_____ **Working by yourself**
_____ **Working with others in groups and teams**
_____ **Building activities (constructing things)**

4. List other things you think you are good at that aren't on the list above:

_____

_____

_____

5. What is your favorite way to learn about things? For example, reading, talking to others, acting things out, hands-on activities, studying alone, etc.

_____

6. Rank yourself in the following intelligences. Use a 1–10 scale with 10 meaning that you are very strong.

Verbal-Linguistic	_____	**Math-Logic**	_____
Spatial	_____	**Bodily-Kinesthetic**	_____
Intrapersonal	_____	**Musical**	_____
Interpersonal	_____	**Naturalist**	_____

7. What skill, activity, or school subject would you most like to improve in?

_____

_____

8. What skill, activity, or school subject do you feel you have improved in?

_____

_____

9. What improvements or changes could be made to make learning more interesting and meaningful for you?

_____

10. What is one of your best memories of school?

_____

11. What are some careers that interest you for your future?

_____

Parent Questionnaire
for MI Assessment

I am in the process of assessing your child's natural talents and strengths in the multiple intelligences areas. Please complete the following questionnaire and return it to me. Your input is highly valuable to this process.

Name _____   Date _____

1. What do you feel is your child's favorite subject in school? _____

2. What are your child's hobbies and interests outside of school?

3. Check all of the things your child is good at:

_____ Reading

_____ Writing

_____ Speaking in front of others or in small groups

_____ Art (drawing, painting, sculpting, etc.)

_____ Music (singing, listening to music, playing an instrument, etc.)

_____ Math (calculating, measuring, solving logic problems, etc.)

_____ Movement Activities (dancing, acting, playing sports, etc.)

_____ Working alone

_____ Working with others in groups and teams

_____ Building activities (constructing things)

4. List other areas in which your child excels that aren't on the list above:

5. What is your child's favorite way to learn about things? For example, reading, talking to others, acting things out, hands-on activities, studying alone, etc.

6. Rank your child in the following intelligences. Use a 1–10 scale (10 being strong).

Verbal-linguistic	_____	Bodily-kinesthetic	_____
Math-logic	_____	Intrapersonal	_____
Spatial	_____	Musical	_____
Interpersonal	_____	Naturalist	_____

7. What skill, activity, or subject would you like to see your child improve in most?

8. What skill, activity, or school subject do you feel your child has improved in?

9. What do you feel your child would you like to learn more about?

10. What improvements or changes could be made to make learning more interesting and meaningful for your child?

11. What is one of your best memories of your child's school life?

12. What careers do you feel may interest your child in the future?

Why? What? Where? When? Who?…Assessment

1. The items I currently use for assessing students' academic achievement include:

2. From my perspective, the purpose of assessment is:

3. I feel that assessment should be expanded or changed in the following ways:

4. The intelligences that most assessments measure use:

5. I would like to expand my assessment measures to include:

6. I can use my dominant intelligences to strengthen my assessment measures in the following ways:

Teacher Reflection Inventory

This teaching inventory is designed to help you reflect on your personal teaching style. After filling out the inventory, review it to see which intelligences you are strong in and which offer challenges. Pay close attention to those areas of instruction you may neglect because of your individual strengths and weaknesses. Discuss your intelligences with a colleague and ask what he or she thinks are your strong intelligences.

1. My personal intelligence strengths include:

2. The subjects and lessons I teach typically include the following intelligences. (Is there any correlation with your answers in #1?)

3. The intelligences I enjoy most in my students are:

4. Intelligences I usually overlook in my teaching are:

5. It would be easier to teach through these overlooked intelligences if:

6. Resources for enhancing my teaching by bringing in these overlooked intelligences would include:

References

Armstrong, Thomas. *Awakening Your Child's Natural Genius: Enhancing Curiosity, Creativity, and Learning Ability.* New York: The Putnam Publishing Group, 1991.

Armstrong, Thomas. *In Their Own Way: Discovering and Encouraging Your Child's Personal Learning Style.* Los Angeles: Jeremy P. Tarcher, Inc., 1987.

Armstrong, Thomas. *Multiple Intelligences in the Classroom.* Alexandria Virginia: Association for Supervision and Curriculum Development, 1994.

Armstrong, Thomas. *7 Kinds of Smart: Identifying and Developing Your Many Intelligences.* New York: Plume, Penguin Group, 1993.

Bates, D. and Keirsey, D. *Please Understand Me: Character and Temperament Types.* California: Prometheus Nemesis Book Company, 1984.

Bellanca, J. and Fogarty, R. *Multiple Intelligences: A Collection.* Illinois: IRI/Skylight Publishing, 1995.

Bruetsch, Anne. *Multiple Intelligences Lesson Plan Book.* Arizona: Zephyr Press, 1995.

Callahan-Young, S. and O'Connor, A. *Seven Windows to a Child's World: 100 Ideas for the Multiple Intelligences Classroom.* Illinois: IRI/Skylight Publishing, 1994.

Campbell, Bruce. *The Multiple Intelligences Handbook: Lesson Plans and More.* Washington: Campbell and Assoc, 1994.

Campbell, B. and Dickinson, D. *Teaching and Learning Through Multiple Intelligences.* Washington: New Horizons for Learning, 1992.

Chapman, Carolyn. *If the Shoe Fits: How to Develop Multiple Intelligences in the Classroom.* Illinois: IRI/Skylight Publishing, 1993.

Csikszentmihalyi, Mihaly. *Flow.* New York: Harper and Row, 1990.

Faculty of New City School. *Celebrating Multiple Intelligences: Teaching for Success. A Practical Guide Created by the Faculty of the New City School.* St. Louis, MO: The New City School, Inc., 1994.

Gardner, Howard. *Creating Minds.* New York: BasicBooks, HarperCollins Publishers, 1993.

Gardner, Howard. *Frames of Mind: The Theory of Multiple Intelligences.* New York: BasicBooks, HarperCollins Publishers, 1985.

Gardner, Howard. *Multiple Intelligences:The Theory in Practice.* New York: BasicBooks, HarperCollins Publishers, 1993.

Gardner, Howard. *The Unschooled Mind: How Children Think and How Schools Should Teach.* New York: BasicBooks, 1991.

Goleman, Daniel. *Emotional Intelligence.* New York: Bantam Books, 1995.

Haggerty, Brian. *Nurturing Intelligences: A Guide to Multiple Intelligences Theory and Teaching.* California: Innovative Learning, Addison-Wesley Publishing Company, 1995.

James, Jennifer. *Thinking in the Future Tense: Leadership Skills for a New Age.* New York: Simon and Shuster, 1996.

Jensen, Eric. *The Learning Brain.* San Diego: Turning Point for Teachers, 1994.

Jorgensen, G. and Wood, B. *A Treasure Chest for Teachers and Children Too: Themes to Foster Multiple Intelligences.* Heads Together, Dalby, Queensland, Australia: Heads Together (available through Zephyr Press), 1994.

Kovalik, Susan. *ITI: The Model - Integrated Thematic Instruction.* Washington: Books for Educators, 1993.

Lazear, David. *Multiple Intelligence Approaches to Assessment: Solving the Assessment Conundrum.* Arizona: Zephyr Press, 1994.

Lazear, David. *Seven Pathways of Learning: Teaching Students and Parents About Multiple Intelligences.* Tucson: Zephyr Press, 1994.

Lazear, David. *Seven Ways of Knowing: Understanding Multiple Intelligences. 2nd Ed.* David. Illinois: Skylight Publishing, 1991.

Lazear, David. *Seven Ways of Teaching: The Artistry of Teaching With Multiple Intelligences.* Illinois: Skylight Publishing, 1991.

Majoy, Peter. *Doorways to Learning; A Model for Developing the Brain's Full Potential.* Arizona: Zephyr Press, 1993.

Margulies, Nancy. *The Magic 7: Tools for Building Your Multiple Intelligences.* (Interactive Comics, Vol. 2) Arizona: Zephyr Press, 1995.

Rose, Colin. *Accelerated Learning.* New York: Dell Publishing, 1985.

Routman, Regie. *Invitations: Changing as Teachers and Learners K–12.* Toronto, Canada: Irwin Publishing, 1991.

Sitton, Rebecca. *Spelling Sourcebook 1: Your Guide for Developing Research-Based Spelling Instruction for the Writing-Rich Classroom.* Washington: Rebecca Sitton Egger Publishing, 1995.

Sylwester, Robert. *A Celebration of Neurons. An Educator's Guide to the Human Brain.* Alexandria, Virginia: Association for Supervision and Curriculum Development, 1995.

Trelease, Jim. *The Read-Aloud Handbook.* New York: Penguin Books, 1985.

Walker, Rena. *Accelerating Literacy: A Handbook to Assist Educators in Creating Balanced Literacy Instruction.* San Diego: Walker Enterprises, 1995.